PANDEMIC PREPAREDNESS AND RESPONSE STRATEGIES

COVID-19 LESSONS FROM THE REPUBLIC OF KOREA, THAILAND, AND VIET NAM

Patrick L. Osewe

OCTOBER 2021

ASIAN DEVELOPMENT BANK

ADB

© 2021 Asian Development Bank
6 ADB Avenue, Mandaluyong City, 1550 Metro Manila, Philippines
Tel +63 2 8632 4444; Fax +63 2 8636 2444
www.adb.org

Some rights reserved. Published in 2021.

ISBN 978-92-9269-074-8 (print); 978-92-9269-075-5 (electronic); 978-92-9269-076-2 (ebook)
Publication Stock No. TCS210037
DOI: http://dx.doi.org/10.22617/TCS210037

Notes:
In this publication, "$" refers to United States dollars, "B" to baht, and "W" to won.
ADB recognizes "Korea" and "South Korea" as the Republic of Korea and "Laos" as the Lao People's Democratic Republic.

On the cover: The coronavirus disease (COVID-19) pandemic has underscored the importance of strong and resilient health systems, including universal health coverage and basic public health measures. It has also emphasized the pivotal role of innovation, such as digital health, in pandemic response. All these have proven to be necessary in coping with and addressing the impacts of COVID-19.

Cover design by Michael Cortes.

Contents

Tables, Figures, and Boxes

Foreword

The coronavirus disease (COVID-19) pandemic has impacted nearly every country in the world. As of October 2021, more than 200 million cases have been registered worldwide and the mounting global death toll well exceeds 4 million people. While the trajectory of the pandemic has unfolded in numerous ways around the globe, social and economic progress, healthcare, education, and the livelihoods of tens of millions of people have been disrupted, and in many cases, irrevocably reversed. Furthermore, the brunt of these effects has fallen disproportionately on vulnerable populations, with existing gaps between rich and poor notably exacerbated. In short, the global pandemic has reshaped everyday life for many of us and it threatens to further intensify inequalities in communities across the world.

The pandemic has also highlighted stark differences in the capacities of health systems to cope with a public health emergency of this scale. Countries in the Asia and Pacific region, in particular, have demonstrated a wide range of responses to the pandemic, with varied public health approaches, leadership tactics, and political dynamics factoring into a country's efficacy and level of success. For example, while some countries imposed strict lockdowns, others kept their borders and economic activities open. Some countries acted early and aggressively and managed to mitigate widespread community transmission, while delays in other countries resulted in an incoherent response strategy. At the same time, some countries opted for a top–down approach while others aimed to establish public trust through the communication of scientific evidence. Through these varied experiences, a number of lessons have been learned about outbreak response interventions, the role of health systems and health systems strengthening in pandemic preparedness, and the complex factors that influence a country's response strategy.

Within this context, the Health Sector Group of the Asian Development Bank (ADB) presents this publication highlighting successful COVID-19 responses from three countries within the Asia and Pacific region. Each case study provides an overview of the country's health system and pandemic preparedness efforts, along with those factors, strategies, mechanisms, and innovations that were identified as most successful in supporting COVID-19 response efforts. It describes how governments engaged across and within sectors, including with civil society and the private sector, to mount a more coherent and effective response.

As we look forward to the rollout of vaccines to wider segments of the global population—and hopefully significantly fewer COVID-19 deaths—we also recognize that the lessons and successes captured herein remain significant. The pandemic is not over and vaccines will not be available in many parts of the world in 2021. Therefore, countries must remain vigilant and continue to adopt and adapt those strategies that have proven most effective.

ADB remains committed to supporting its developing member countries accelerate their responses and contributing to the global collective action required to end this pandemic as swiftly as possible.

Bruno Carrasco
Director General concurrently Chief Compliance Officer
Sustainable Development and Climate Change Department
Asian Development Bank

Acknowledgments

The case studies in this publication were written by Patrick Osewe, Chief of Health Sector Group at the Asian Development Bank (ADB). Consultants Nansubuga Isdahl, Michael Peters, and Vas Yiengprugsawan contributed invaluable support. The case studies benefited from reviews and feedback of ADB staff in country offices and Ministry of Health officials in Thailand and Viet Nam.

Valuable inputs were also provided by the World Health Organization's Western Pacific Region Office (WPRO) representatives. Finally, special thanks are owed to ADB's Department of Communications for their assistance in the publication process.

Abbreviations

ADB	Asian Development Bank
CCSA	Centre for COVID-19 Situation Administration
CDSC HQ	Central Disaster and Safety Countermeasures Headquarters
COVID-19	coronavirus disease
CSMBS	Civil Servant Medical Benefit Scheme
GDP	gross domestic product
ICT	information and communication technology
JEE	Joint External Evaluation
KCDC	Korea Centers for Disease Control and Prevention
H5N1	avian influenza
IHR	International Health Regulations
MERS	Middle East Respiratory Syndrome
MFA	Ministry of Foreign Affairs
MOPH	Ministry of Public Health
NCD	noncommunicable diseases
NHI	national health insurance
NHSO	National Health Security Office
OECD	Organisation for Economic Co-operation and Development
OOP	out-of-pocket
PHC	primary health care
PRC	People's Republic of China
ROK	Republic of Korea
SARS	severe acute respiratory syndrome
SDG	Sustainable Development Goal
UHC	universal health coverage
VHV	village health volunteer
WHO	World Health Organization

Introduction

More than one and a half years after the pandemic was declared (as of 18 October 2021), the coronavirus disease (COVID-19) has claimed nearly 5 million lives around the world and infected hundreds of millions of people.[1] Recognizing its sheer magnitude, the United Nations, scientists, and other experts have declared COVID-19 the "greatest public health crisis in living memory."[2] Indeed, over the past year, it has left an unforgettable mark on the world and will likely lead to lasting shifts in how communities and countries view public health and safety.

Aside from the tragic death toll in 2020, COVID-19 plunged the global economy into its worst recession since World War II,[3] pushed millions into poverty, reversed gains in human development and progress toward the Sustainable Development Goals (SDGs),[4] and contributed to increased domestic abuse and mental health issues.[5] Given the unprecedented nature of the crisis, the full scale and scope of COVID-19 is still unknown—including both its role as an accelerant of emergent trends (i.e., digital transformation), as well as its negative impact on existing inequalities.

A significant milestone in the fight against the pandemic was achieved in December 2020 when the United Kingdom and the United States approved several long-awaited vaccines for emergency use. However, global efforts to procure and distribute vaccines to vulnerable populations remain a mammoth task. Due in part to logistical/manufacturing challenges and inequalities in vaccine access, some groups estimate that many low-income countries might not be able to vaccinate their populations until 2023 or 2024.[6] As a result, nonpharmaceutical public health interventions will likely remain critical for curbing the spread of COVID-19 through 2021 and for the foreseeable future. Countries must remain vigilant in their response efforts, adapting them as necessary to prevent and control further outbreaks.

Amidst these extraordinary circumstances, it has become clear that many of the pandemic-related challenges faced by communities, societies, and countries are complex and interconnected. For example, COVID-19 has demonstrated the inextricable linkages between human wellbeing and economic development—both through the challenges laid bare by fragile public health systems and the successes of those countries with universal health coverage (UHC), where all people have access to the health services they need without incurring financial hardship. What has also become clear is that the

---

1   Center for Systems Science and Engineering (CSSE) at Johns Hopkins University. 2021. COVID-19 Dashboard. https://coronavirus.jhu.edu/map. html (accessed 11 March 2021).

2   United Nations. 2020. Everyone, Everywhere Must Have Access to Eventual COVID-19 Immunization, Secretary-General Says in Video Message for Global Vaccine Summit. Press release. 4 June. https://www.un.org/press/en/2020/sgsm20108.doc.htm.

3   The World Bank. 2020. COVID-19 to Plunge Global Economy into Worst Recession since World War II. Press release. 8 June. https://www.worldbank.org/en/news/press-release/2020/06/08/covid-19-to-plunge-global-economy-into-worst-recession-since-world-war-ii.

4   United Nations Department of Economic and Social Affairs. 2020. UN report finds COVID-19 is reversing decades of progress on poverty, healthcare and education. News release. 7 July. https://www.un.org/development/desa/en/news/sustainable/sustainable-development-goals-report-2020.html and United Nations. 2020. The Sustainable Development Goals Report. New York.

5   V. Bhavsar et. al. 2021. Lockdown, Domestic Abuse Perpetration, and Mental Health Care: Gaps in Training, Research, and Policy. The Lancet Psychiatry. 8(3). pp. 172–174.

6   Duke Global Health Institute. 2020. Will Low-Income Countries Be Left Behind When COVID-19 Vaccines Arrive? News release. 9 November. https://globalhealth.duke.edu/news/will-low-income-countries-be-left-behind-when-covid-19-vaccines-arrive.

pandemic has been most successfully contained in those countries where diverse expertise, multiple sectors, and a broad spectrum of actors have been meaningfully involved in decision-making and response activities.

Across the world, promising examples have emerged of how governments and health systems are boosting capacities, innovating local solutions, and strategically realigning themselves to respond to the impacts of the pandemic. In Asia and the Pacific, the region where COVID-19 originated, many countries reacted swiftly and aggressively—bringing to the forefront a range of good practices and lessons learned in emergency and crisis planning, management, coordination, and response.

Although countries within Asia and the Pacific have varied widely in terms of their level of COVID-19 response, a number of them have successfully adapted and implemented mitigation measures to their contexts—from the success of the Republic of Korea (ROK) with testing and digital contact tracing to Thailand, leveraging a network of more than one million community workers to support the prevention, detection, and reporting of COVID-19. In Viet Nam, a focus on prevention, significant investment in public health infrastructure, and public solidarity enabled the country of 100 million people to register fewer than 2,000 total COVID-19 cases from the start of the pandemic until December 2020.

Within this context, the Asian Development Bank (ADB) set out to capture and assess a range of COVID-19 response and recovery efforts across the region—including success stories, challenges, and the associated contributing factors—with particular focus on understanding and explaining how progress was achieved across diverse settings. Given what is now known about COVID-19, these case studies aim to provide the global community with insights into the successes, opportunities, and challenges in delivering innovative and robust responses to fight the pandemic. They may be useful both as countries refine their COVID-19 response efforts and improve their overall pandemic preparedness (e.g., many countries that had the virus under control have witnessed new outbreaks intermittently), and in light of the challenges that lie ahead in vaccine roll-out.

Therefore, the purpose of this publication is to share experiences in addressing COVID-19 across three distinct countries: the ROK, Thailand, and Viet Nam. The three case studies presented in this publication reflect just a few of the many pathways and models that countries in the region have used to combat the pandemic. A synthesis of common, cross-cutting themes found among all case studies is also included in the conclusion section of this compilation to enhance overall learning.

Specific objectives of this publication include:

- describing the factors/strategies that were most successful in supporting COVID-19 response efforts and under what circumstances they took place;
- highlighting the role of UHC and robust health systems in strengthening pandemic response;
- documenting how governments, civil society, communities, the private sector, and other partners worked together in planning and executing COVID-19 response actions; and
- promoting knowledge sharing.

It must be emphasized that the case studies of good practices presented here are not exhaustive, nor are they conclusive. While they each include comprehensive information on the specific epidemiological dynamics of the country, the aim of the case studies was not to reflect the entire scope of a country's COVID-19 response efforts but rather to provide specific examples of *key factors* that supported response, as well as to identify any commonalties across the region. Due to limited resources and time, it was not possible to include a larger sample of countries. The countries were selected based on a range of factors, including COVID-19 burden, geographical and income representation, and progress in implementing UHC systems. Further, due to the rapidly shifting nature of the pandemic, information may have evolved from the time of writing.

Information for the case studies was collected through secondary research, including a review of published and unpublished literature, government websites and documentation, data available during the period of writing, as well as interviews with key informants from health and finance ministries. Preliminary findings from these case studies were presented in

September 2020 at ADB's Joint Ministers of Finance and Health Symposium on Universal Health Coverage in Asia and the Pacific: COVID-19 and Beyond and incorporate feedback received from regional World Health Organization offices. The final cases were reviewed by government stakeholders and ADB's country offices when possible.

This collection of case studies demonstrates that a range of successful responses to COVID-19 can be applied in diverse settings, including high- and low-resource contexts, and that no single path leads to success. At the same time, the cases share many of the same lessons. These commonalities serve to illuminate areas where decision makers in other countries may focus attention. Ultimately, ADB hopes the lessons in these case studies can enhance efforts to mitigate and build resilience against public health disasters and outbreaks—especially as the world will likely continue to face challenges in responding to COVID-19 and other emerging infectious diseases in 2021 and beyond.

Table 1: Selected Indicators by Country

Country	Republic of Korea	Thailand	Viet Nam
Population	51.7 million	69.6 million	96.4 million
Income status (World Bank 2019 classification)	High	Upper middle	Lower middle
Region	East Asia	Southeast Asia	Southeast Asia
Type of government	Centralized democratic republic	Centralized unitary parliamentary constitutional monarchy	Centralized unitary republic
Total COVID-19 cases (as of 17 Dec 2020)	46,453	4,281	1,407
Total COVID-19 deaths (as of 17 Dec 2020)	634	60	35

COVID-19 = coronavirus disease.

Sources: Center for Systems Science and Engineering (CSSE) at Johns Hopkins University. 2021. COVID-19 Dashboard. https://coronavirus.jhu.edu/map.html (accessed 17 December 2020); and World Bank. 2020. World Development Indicators. https://data.worldbank.org/ (accessed 17 December 2020).

1 Republic of Korea

Executive Summary

The Republic of Korea's (ROK's) first positive case of the coronavirus disease (COVID-19) was confirmed on 20 January 2020, soon after the initial outbreak in Wuhan, People's Republic of China (PRC). As case counts rose—peaking at 909 new daily confirmed cases on 29 February 2020—the government quickly mounted a rapid and efficient response that supported the country to successfully control the first outbreak within a month of its peak.[1] Informed by previous pandemic experience, a crisp strategic direction, and decisive leadership, the ROK bent the curve of infections downward without implementing widespread lockdowns. Despite two spikes in cases since February (in May and August), the country successfully managed to keep the virus under control. As of 24 November 2020, the country had reported 31,353 confirmed cases of COVID-19 and 510 deaths.[2]

The ROK's success in blunting the impact of COVID-19 reflects significant investments in its public health system, including its ability to apply lessons learned after recent infectious disease outbreaks. The entire population of the ROK is insured, with approximately 97% insured through the country's universal healthcare system.[3] Total healthcare spending was 7.6% of gross domestic product (GDP) in 2017, of which public health expenditure was 4.4% of GDP.[4] The country has both a high number of hospital beds per capita and a high universal health coverage (UHC) service coverage index (Sustainable Development Goal [SDG] 3.8.1), at 85.7, among the highest in the region.[5] Recent outbreaks of infectious diseases Severe Acute Respiratory Syndrome (SARS) in 2003 and Middle East Respiratory Syndrome (MERS) in 2015 revealed weaknesses in the country's preparedness for emerging infectious diseases that prompted reforms to the country's system for preparing and responding to infectious diseases. Many of these reforms are reflected in the country's actions to curtail the spread of COVID-19 and are described below.

Investing in preparedness

Recent outbreaks prompted the government to reassess its preparedness for public health emergencies and further reinforce the resilience of its health system. Specifically, after the country's experience with MERS, the government made a concerted effort to strengthen their capabilities and systems for public health emergency response—allocating more funding to the Korea Disease Control and Prevention Agency, formerly the Korea Centers for Disease Control and Prevention, strengthening surveillance systems, increasing the number of professional epidemiological investigators, improving hospital infection prevention and control, improving diagnostic testing capabilities by enlisting

1 Government of the Republic of Korea. 2020. *How Korea Responded to a Pandemic using ICT Flattening the Curve on COVID-19*. https://overseas.mofa.go.kr/gr-en/brd/m_6940/view.do?seq=761548&srchFr=&amp%253BsrchTo=&amp%253BsrchWord=&amp%253BsrchTp=&amp%253Bmulti_itm_seq=0&amp%253Bitm_seq_1=0&amp%253Bitm_seq_2=0&amp%253Bcompany_cd=&aSeoul.

2 Center for Systems Science and Engineering (CSSE) at Johns Hopkins University. 2021. COVID-19 Dashboard. https://coronavirus.jhu.edu/map.html (accessed 24 November 2020).

3 World Health Organization (WHO). Regional Office for the Western Pacific. 2015. *Republic of Korea Health System Review*. Manila.

4 WHO. 2020. Global Health Expenditure Database. https://apps.who.int/nha/database (accessed 10 September 2020).

5 WHO. 2019. *Primary Health Care on the Road to Universal Health Coverage*. Geneva.

the private sector, and revising public health legislation to fast-track authorizations and enable comprehensive contact tracing. Prior investments in digital health data infrastructure and data analytics proved invaluable in guiding decision making.

Executing clearsighted strategies with agility

Early on, the ROK made the simple decision to test and trace as many people as possible. The government's rapid but clearsighted leadership enabled the country to then maximize its existing capacity and investments. Once this strategic focus was laid out, it was enhanced through a number of innovations such as the rapid development of test kits, drive-through testing facilities, and a restructuring of triage and treatment. Furthermore, centralized leadership and coordination with active cooperation across subnational levels of government, helped to facilitate the government's agile and adaptive response.

Harnessing data and technology

Building on its dynamic digital infrastructure and information and communication technology (ICT) sector, along with revised legislation following MERS that enabled real-time contact tracing, authorities swiftly deployed digital tools and solutions to contain COVID-19. This included the use of big data and artificial intelligence that enabled the rapid development of test kits; linked location, surveillance, and transaction data; self-diagnosis applications to monitor symptoms; and mobile applications to provide real-time information on locations visited by patients diagnosed with COVID-19.

The case of the ROK demonstrates how long-term investments in and prioritization of public health systems, including UHC, combined with clear leadership and public trust can coalesce to create an effective national strategy. However, what underpins the country's response actions is not only that they reflected the strategic importance of health systems strengthening, but also that they were activated quickly and simultaneously. This was largely possible due to systematic and deliberate investments across the health system (e.g., diagnostics, infection control, and health data) and between public and private sectors. Thus, as the COVID-19 crisis continues to evolve, the ROK's strategies—although specific to their context—can, it is hoped, shed light on the vital role that investments in public health systems play in safeguarding health and economic security.

Introduction

The ROK's first positive case of COVID-19 was confirmed on 20 January 2020, soon after the initial outbreak in Wuhan, PRC. As case counts rose—peaking at 909, new daily confirmed cases on 29 February 2020—the ROK faced the worst COVID-19 outbreak outside the PRC, with thousands of cases linked to a church in Daegu city.[6] The government quickly mounted a rapid and efficient response that supported the country to successfully control the first outbreak within a month of its peak (footnote 1). Informed by previous pandemic experience, a crisp strategic direction, and decisive leadership, the ROK bent the curve of infections downward without implementing widespread lockdowns. After the peak of the pandemic, daily cases remained largely in the double-digits, with the exception of two spikes. One occurred in mid-May as the country started to reopen and another in late August following 9 days of triple-digit increases. On 22 August 2020, the country reported close to 400 cases tied to another church in northern Seoul—the highest daily jump in cases since March 2020.[7] While cases were reported to quickly spread across the country's major cities and provinces, the resurgence has since been suppressed.

Amidst this evolving context, this case study provides an overview of the ROK's vigorous efforts to curtail the virus. Specifically, it describes how through a number of systems-wide strategic efforts and previous investments in health emergency preparedness, the country has interrupted the spread of COVID-19 and limited deaths.

---

[6]   J. Oh et al. 2020. National Response to COVID-19 in the Republic of Korea and Lessons Learned for Other Countries. *Health Systems and Reform*. (6)1. https://pubmed.ncbi.nlm.nih.gov/32347772/.

[7]   H. Kim. 2020. South Korea Warns of 'Massive' Coronavirus Risk. *Bloomberg*. News release. 23 August. https://www.bloomberg.com/news/articles/2020-08-23/jump-in-seoul-s-covid-19-cases-sparks-fear-of-nationwide-spread.

Background

Country context

The ROK has experienced unparalleled economic growth since the latter half of the 20th century. The country's rapid industrialization began to accelerate in the 1960s with a number of policy reforms—including the shift to a manufacturing-led economy. As a result, the ROK is now one of the world's most developed economies, with a GDP per capita of $42,925 in 2019.[8] The country's economic gains were matched by the expansion of healthcare and a marked improvement in health indicators. Life expectancy at birth rose by 17 years from 1960 to 1990, while infant mortality dropped from 80 deaths per 1,000 births to 13 during the same period.[9]

Health system

Health policy and planning is led by the Ministry of Health and Welfare at the national level. Subnationally, regional governments oversee regional delivery systems, including regional medical centers, according to local context and needs, while municipalities manage public health services through health centers, health subcenters, and primary health care posts (footnote 3). The entire population of the ROK is insured, with approximately 97% of its 51.7 million citizens insured through the country's UHC system—a result of the country's adoption of both UHC in 1989 and a single-payer system in 2000 (footnote 3)—and the remaining 3% wholly covered by government subsidies. The ROK's health system relies largely on finance through the national health insurance (NHI) and approximately 90% of medical facilities are private.[10] The NHI has two quasi-governmental agencies: the National Health Insurance Service, which manages the program; and the Health Insurance Review and Assessment Service, which reviews the care covered by it, including overseeing reimbursements, medical claims, and quality assessments (footnote 10).

The government's budget allocation in total health expenditure is slightly lower than average spending among Organisation for Economic Co-operation and Development (OECD) countries. As a percentage of GDP, total healthcare spending was 7.6% of GDP in 2017, of which public health expenditure was 4.4% of GDP (footnote 10). The country's health infrastructure includes a high number of hospital beds per capita—at 12.3 beds per 1,000 population—along with 254 healthcare centers, 1,335 subhealth centers, 1,905 primary healthcare posts, and 46 community health promotion centers across the country, as of 2018 (footnote 10). This extensive infrastructure has contributed to the ROK's high UHC service coverage index (SDG 3.8.1), at 85.7, among the highest in the region.[11] Significant investments in health data and technology have also been made. However, the health system does face challenges. Despite universal coverage, out-of-pocket (OOP) payments remain high, with 34.3% of health spending paid as OOP in 2017 (footnote 10). Incidence of catastrophic health expenditure at 10% of household total consumption (SDG goal 3.8.2) was high at 21.8% in 2015 (footnote 11). In addition, demand for hospital-centered care has undermined the establishment of the primary care sector, which is not well established, and has overburdened the NHI system, leading to inefficiencies in health spending and inequities in resource allocation.[12]

Pandemic preparedness

The ROK's success in blunting the impact of COVID-19 reflects significant investments in its public health system, including its ability to apply lessons learned after recent infectious disease outbreaks.

---

8   Organisation for Economic Co-operation and Development (OECD). https://data.oecd.org/korea.htm (accessed 24 September 2020).

9   World Bank. 2020. World Development Indicators. https://data.worldbank.org/indicator/SP.DYN.IMRT.IN?end=1990&locations=KR&start=1960 (accessed 24 September 2020).

10 OECD. 2020. *OECD Reviews of Public Health: Korea: A Healthier Tomorrow*. Paris.

11 WHO. 2019. *Primary Health Care on the Road to Universal Health Coverage: 2019 Global Monitoring Report*. Geneva. https://www.who.int/healthinfo/universal_health_coverage/report/uhc_report_2019.pdf.

12 Y. Cho et al. 2020. Comparison of Patient Perceptions of Primary Care Quality Across Healthcare Facilities in Korea: A Cross-Sectional Study. *PLoS ONE* 15 (3). https://journals.plos.org/plosone/article?id=10.1371/journal.pone.0230034.

Following the SARS outbreak in 2003, the country launched the Korea Centers for Disease Control and Prevention (KCDC)—the agency responsible for preparing for and responding to infectious disease outbreaks. In 2007, the Division of Public Health Crisis Response in KCDC was established to lead the national efforts to respond to emerging infectious diseases.[13]

Since then, the country has further strengthened its public health emergency mechanisms, largely in response to an outbreak of MERS in 2015.[14] The aftermath of the MERS outbreak—during which the ROK experienced the largest number of cases outside the Middle East (186 confirmed cases and 38 deaths)[15] and huge economic losses—revealed weaknesses in the country's preparedness for emerging infectious diseases and prompted government action. Findings from an expert panel that reviewed the country's response identified the government's failure to share information transparently and inefficiencies in the country's infectious disease control system as major contributors to the outbreak's spread.[16] Recommendations from the panel—along with heavy public criticism of the government's response—sparked 48 reforms to the country's system for preparing and responding to infectious diseases.[17]

Broadly, through these reforms, the government took great strides to strengthen its infectious disease surveillance, preparedness, and response capacity and revise relevant legislation. Specifically, the Infectious Disease Control and Prevention Act (2009) was updated in 2015, providing the central government more authority in public health emergencies. These revisions aimed to strengthen coordination between agencies, increase human resources, and improve hospital regulation. Notably, they also allowed for increased information sharing by the government and improvements in the infectious disease surveillance system (footnote 10). The capacity of the KCDC was enhanced through additional funding and recruitment of epidemiologists, and rapid-response teams were established at the provincial level, thereby increasing the capacity for pandemic preparedness at the subnational level.

The KCDC also established both the Center for Public Health Emergency Preparedness and Response, which oversees implementation of the International Health Regulations (IHR) 2005,[18] and the Department of Risk Communication, which plans risk communication activities, including determining what information is shared with the public and how to do so quickly and transparently. In addition, in response to demands to strengthen event-based surveillance, detection, and response capabilities in the initial phase of a public health emergency, the country established a 24-hour Emergency Operations Center under the authority of the KCDC, which collects and monitors information on infectious diseases in real time.[19]

Furthermore, a special task force in charge of emergency management—the Central Disaster and Safety Countermeasures Headquarters (CDSC HQ)—was established under the KCDC (Figure 1.1). Headed by the Prime Minister, the CDSC HQ is responsible for planning and directing the pandemic response, with technical support and guidance from the KCDC. The KCDC leads coordination with provincial and municipal

---

[13]   H.Y. Lee et al. 2013. Public Health Crisis Preparedness and Response in Korea. *Osong Public Health and Research Perspectives.* 4 (5). pp. 278–284. https://www.ncbi.nlm.nih.gov/pmc/articles/PMC3845460/.

[14]   H. Kim. 2020. The Sociopolitical Context of the COVID-19 Response in South Korea. *BMJ Global Health* 5 (5). https://www.ncbi.nlm.nih.gov/pmc/articles/PMC7228497/.

[15]   Korea Centers for Disease Control and Prevention. 2015. Middle East Respiratory Syndrome Coronavirus Outbreak in the Republic of Korea, 2015. *Osong Public Health and Research Perspectives.* Volume 6, Issue 4. pp. 269–278. https://reader.elsevier.com/reader/sd/pii/S2210909916300315?token=0349CC3A00DDEBF2C9ECD553513AE4F8B28D981B7FAE923BF503FAB14B1CBCDDCA1F45B5F560E9530280003823C7A3C4&originRegion=us-east-1&originCreation=20210730195406.

[16]   C. Hang-Sun. 2020. Experts Fault South Korean Response to MERS Outbreak. *New York Times.* 13 June. https://www.nytimes.com/2015/06/14/world/asia/experts-fault-south-korean-response-to-mers-outbreak.html.

[17]   J. Kang et al. 2020. South Korea's Responses to Stop the COVID-19 Pandemic. *American Journal of Infection Control.* 48 (9). pp. 1080–1086.

[18]   WHO. 2018. *Joint External Evaluation of IHR Core Capacities of the Republic of Korea Mission Report.* https://www.who.int/publications/i/item/WHO-WHE-CPI-2017.65.

[19]   D. Ladner, K. Hamaguchi, and K. Kim. 2020. The Republic of Korea's First 70 Days of Responding to the COVID-19 Outbreak. *Global Delivery Initiative.* https://www.effectivecooperation.org/system/files/2021-06/case_study_of_korea_response_to_covid19.pdf.

Figure 1.1: The Response System of the Government of the Republic of Korea—
Red Alert Level IV

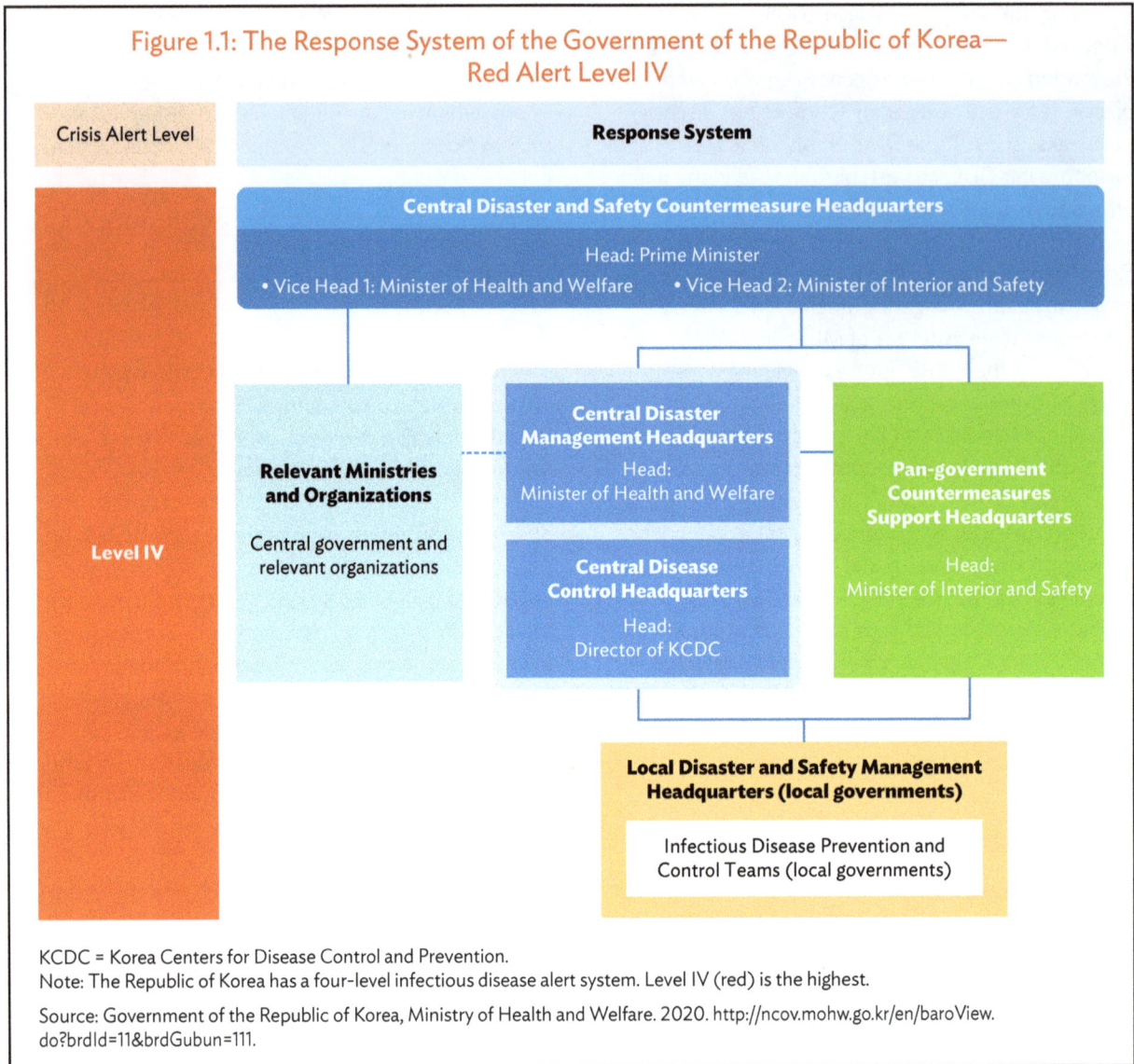

Crisis Alert Level	Response System

Central Disaster and Safety Countermeasure Headquarters

Head: Prime Minister
• Vice Head 1: Minister of Health and Welfare • Vice Head 2: Minister of Interior and Safety

Level IV

Relevant Ministries and Organizations

Central government and relevant organizations

Central Disaster Management Headquarters

Head:
Minister of Health and Welfare

Central Disease Control Headquarters

Head:
Director of KCDC

Pan-government Countermeasures Support Headquarters

Head:
Minister of Interior and Safety

Local Disaster and Safety Management Headquarters (local governments)

Infectious Disease Prevention and Control Teams (local governments)

KCDC = Korea Centers for Disease Control and Prevention.
Note: The Republic of Korea has a four-level infectious disease alert system. Level IV (red) is the highest.

Source: Government of the Republic of Korea, Ministry of Health and Welfare. 2020. http://ncov.mohw.go.kr/en/baroView.do?brdId=11&brdGubun=111.

governments and specialized hospitals, while local units were established to coordinate with central authorities.[20]

The country's efforts to strengthen its pandemic preparedness capacities are also reflected in its commitment to meeting the IHR (2005) requirements for health security. In 2017, the ROK participated in a joint review of its IHR core capacities using the Joint External Evaluation (JEE) process of the World Health Organization (WHO). Findings from the JEE process highlighted the country's strong systems and capacities for addressing pandemics, disasters, and public health emergencies, but also a need to prioritize public health risks and strengthen risk communication, among other areas (footnote 18). Furthermore, in July 2018, a government-wide research and development fund aimed at investing in vaccines, therapeutics, and diagnostics for infectious diseases was launched (initially funded with $32.5 million over 5 years).[21]

---

[20] Government of the Republic of Korea. 2020. *COVID-19 Response*. http://ncov.mohw.go.kr/en/baroView.do?brdId=11&brdGubun=111&dataGubun=&ncvContSeq=&contSeq=&board_id=.

[21] Right Fund. 2020. *RIGHT Fund Expands Support for Infectious Diseases Research. March.* http://www.rightfund.org/en/2020/03/10/right-fund-expands-support-for-infectious-diseases-research/.

The government response to pandemics has remained nimble, as recent actions to strengthen pandemic response systems have demonstrated. In December 2019, approximately 1 month before the country's first reported case of COVID-19, public health experts conducted a desktop exercise on emergency responses to a mysterious outbreak of an unidentified disease contracted by a family after traveling to the PRC. As a result of this exercise, KCDC experts developed algorithm and testing techniques, both of which were mobilized when the first suspected case of COVID-19 was identified in January 2020.[22]

As the ROK initiated its response to COVID-19 virus, the combination of these efforts enabled the country to mount a strong frontline defense with the following strategies distinguishing its actions.

COVID-19 in the Republic of Korea

Overall transmission dynamics

The ROK's first case of COVID-19 was imported from Wuhan (PRC) and identified on 20 January 2020. In the weeks that followed, the number of confirmed cases remained low—averaging one to two per day. A surge in cases was detected on 19 February after which the epicenter of the outbreak was identified through a cluster tied to a church in the city of Daegu, southeast of Seoul.[23] The cluster in Daegu—considered a superspreading event—was linked to the virus' rapid surge in the country and resulted in more than 5,000 cases.

As the ROK initiated its response in early 2020, the government moved fast to raise its alert levels. The country—which had initially declared a yellow alert (caution) after its first case was confirmed on 20 January—declared the highest alert level (red) from its four-level infectious disease alert system on 23 February. Through the red (severe) alert, authority to contain the disease and coordinate response efforts was transferred from the Minister of Health and Welfare to the Prime Minister under the CDSC HQ.[24] The red alert allowed the government to earmark additional funds to fight against the virus and made it easier for health officials to use personal data for contact tracing; controlling air, train, and other public traffic; and outlawing religious and other gatherings.[25] By 29 February, a peak of 909 daily cases had been reached, with the number of new cases declining through the end of March. The country's cases largely remained in the double-digits, with the exception of two spikes in cases. One occurred in mid-May as the country started to reopen and another in mid-to-late August following 9 days of triple-digit increases. On 22 August 2020, the country reported nearly 400 cases tied to another church in northern Seoul—the highest daily jump in cases since March.[26] According to published data, the official national tally of cases included approximately 31,353 confirmed cases of COVID-19 and 510 deaths as of 24 November 2020 (footnote 2).

Detection

The Government of the ROK quickly adopted a widespread testing strategy that included testing asymptomatic individuals. The rollout of rapid diagnostic testing was a key pillar of the country's response and relied largely on the country's ability to quickly develop and manufacture tests. Just 1 week after the country's first case was diagnosed, KCDC officials met with more than 20 private sector partners to discuss mass production of COVID-19

22   H. Shin. 2020. South Korea's Emergency Exercise in December Facilitated Coronavirus Testing, Containment. 30 March. https://www.reuters.com/article/us-health-coronavirus-southkorea-drills/south-koreas-emergency-exercise-in-december-facilitated-coronavirus-testing-containment-idUSKBN21H0BQ.

23   Our World in Data. 2020. *Emerging COVID-19 Success Story: South Korea Learned the Lessons of MERS.* ourworldindata.org/covid-exemplar-south-korea.

24   Government of the Republic of Korea. 2020. *Korean Government's Response System.* 25 February. Press release. http://ncov.mohw.go.kr/en/baroView.do?brdId=11&brdGubun=111&dataGubun=&ncvContSeq=&contSeq=&board_id=&gubun=.

25   C. Sang-Hun. 2020. As Coronavirus Cases Spiral, South Korea Raises Threat Alert Level. *New York Times.* 23 February. https://www.nytimes.com/2020/02/23/world/asia/south-korea-coronavirus-moon.html.

26   H. Kim. 2020. South Korea Warns of 'Massive' Coronavirus Risk. *Bloomberg.* 23 August. https://www.bloomberg.com/news/articles/2020-08-23/jump-in-seoul-s-covid-19-cases-sparks-fear-of-nationwide-spread.

testing kits.[27] The government utilized the Emergency Use Authorization—introduced in the aftermath of the 2015 MERS outbreak—to fast-track approval of quality test kits. Within 1 week, on 4 February, Kogene Biotech was the first company authorized to begin production of testing kits. In early February, testing was expanded with the help of a new, single-step, real-time reverse transcription polymerase chain reaction (RT-PCR) test kit, which produced results in 6 hours.

Initial focus was placed on testing in dangerous hotspots and emerging clusters of disease transmission. As demand for testing increased throughout the country, a number of testing models and sites were made available to the public. Testing services were provided at healthcare facilities, public health centers, walk-in booths, door-to-door visits, and drive-through testing centers. Tests were conducted free of charge, covered by the government and the NHI, and results were sent to mobile phones within 24 hours. Daily testing capacity reached 15,000 by mid-March and by mid-April, more than 600 screening centers could perform diagnostic tests.[28] By the end of April, more than half a million tests were conducted throughout the country.[29]

When members of a religious sect located in Daegu—a city of more than 2.4 million people—started getting sick in February 2020, a cascading number of cases followed and it quickly became the epicenter of the outbreak. A 61-year-old woman, also known as Patient 31 and linked to a megachurch in the city, was believed to have infected many others during two church services. Thereafter, efforts were made to identify all of the people potentially exposed to the virus. By 29 February, more than 2,000 confirmed cases were reported in the city.

By 7 March, more than 5,000 cases were recorded and the city's healthcare system was quickly overwhelmed.[30] The identification of the Daegu clusters prompted the government to rapidly activate a more comprehensive national response in an effort to tamp down transmission (Box 1.1).

Containment

The ROK did not implement a widespread national lockdown to curb the spread of the virus. Instead, alongside extensive testing, the country exercised an aggressive tracking and tracing strategy that included prompt epidemiological investigations to control and contain transmission. Revisions to the country's Infectious Disease Control and Prevention Act after the 2015 MERS outbreak established the basis for a comprehensive digitally-enabled contract tracing strategy (Box 1.2) through which potential contacts with an infected person could be traced and placed in quarantine.[31]

Epidemiological Intelligence Service (EIS) officers (both fully-trained existing officers and a temporary workforce deployed in response to the pandemic) combined information gained through interviews with a number of other data sources—including GPS data, video surveillance, and credit card transactions—to create detailed timelines of individual cases and to trace close contacts of the infected. Contact tracing was facilitated by the COVID-19 Epidemiological Investigation Support System, which the government developed to coordinate and centralize data collection. The newly-developed platform allows the data collected from EIS officers to identify the transmission routes of infected individuals in real-time and within minutes, whereas previous analysis time was 24 hours (footnote 1). Once again, legislation passed in

[27] C. Terhune et al. 2020. Special Report: How Korea Trounced U.S. in Race to Test People for Coronavirus. *Reuters*. 18 March. https://www.reuters.com/article/us-health-coronavirus-testing-specialrep/special-report-how-korea-trounced-u-s-in-race-to-test-people-for-coronavirus-idUSKBN2153BW.

[28] M. Fisher M. and C. Sang-Hun. 2020. How South Korea Flattened the Curve. *New York Times*. 23 March. https://www.nytimes.com/2020/03/23/world/asia/coronavirus-south-korea-flatten-curve.html.

[29] Our World in Data. 2020. COVID-19 Testing by Date. https://ourworldindata.org/grapher/full-list-total-tests-for-covid-19?year=latest&time=2020-02-12..2020-04-30&country=AUS~ECU~IND~IDN~ITA~JPN~KAZ~SEN~SGP~ZAF~KOR~TUR~USA (accessed 2 December 2020).

[30] J.H. Kim et al. 2020. How South Korea Responded to the COVID-19 Outbreak in Daegu. *NEJM Catalyst Innovations in Care Delivery*. 1 (4). 10.1056/CAT.20.0159. https://www.ncbi.nlm.nih.gov/pmc/articles/PMC7390493/.

[31] COVID-19 National Emergency Response Center, Epidemiology and Case Management Team, Korea Centers for Disease Control and Prevention. 2020. Contact Transmission of COVID-19 in South Korea: Novel Investigation Techniques for Tracing Contacts. *Osong Public Health and Research Perspectives*. 11 (1). pp. 60–63. http://doi.org/10.24171/j.phrp.2020.11.1.09. Also see footnote 34.

Box 1.1: How Daegu Quickly Changed Course to Control COVID-19 Transmission

Before the outbreak, hospitals in the Republic of Korea operated on their own to isolate patients suffering from priority infectious agents and there was no national system to stratify patients with an infectious disease according to their risk.[a] As the outbreak in the city of Daegu advanced and the health system became overwhelmed, health officials and the national government worked together to rapidly restructure the triage and treatment systems. A plan was developed to manage patients according to risk. Four categories of COVID-19 patients were classified based on severity of symptoms. Asymptomatic and mild patients were quarantined and monitored in community treatment centers (facilities that the government turned into temporary isolation wards). Patients with moderate and severe symptoms were transferred to designated COVID-19 hospitals, and critically ill patients were hospitalized at emergency medical centers. Furthermore, specific hospitals were designated for non-COVID-19 patients. At the same time, hospitals introduced strict screening, testing, and triage procedures upon facility entry to prevent cross-contamination between those people who might be infected with COVID-19 and those who were not, including health workers. Following KCDC recommendations, hospitals adopted the rigorous use of personal protective equipment and implemented a twice-a-day screening for hospital staff working with COVID-19 patients. Health officials also recruited approximately 2,300 health personnel from other regions. By strategically reorganizing the healthcare system and focusing efforts to minimize risk of COVID-19 infection among healthcare workers, health officials were able to effectively target the limited hospital resources for those who needed them most—reorienting the functioning of the health system around slowing the spread of the disease, reducing cross-contamination, and enhancing patient care.

COVID-19 = coronavirus disease, KCDC = Korea Centers for Disease Control and Prevention.

[a] J.H. Kim et al. 2020. How South Korea Responded to the COVID-19 Outbreak in Daegu. *NEJM Catalysis Innovations in Care Delivery.* 1 (4). pp. 10.1056/ CAT.20.0159. doi:10.1056/CAT.20.0159.

Sources: J.H. Kim et al. 2020. How South Korea Responded to the COVID-19 Outbreak in Daegu. *NEJM Catalysis Innovations in Care Delivery.* 1 (4). pp. 10.1056/CAT.20.0159. doi:10.1056/CAT.20.0159; J. Oh et al. 2020. National Response to COVID-19 in the Republic of Korea and Lessons Learned for Other Countries. *Health Systems & Reform.* 6 (1). e-1753464, DOI: 10.1080/23288604.2020.1753464.

Box 1.2: Digital Health and COVID-19 Response

The Republic of Korea (ROK) Government introduced a number of digital health strategies in their pandemic response.

- **Test kits** were rapidly developed using high performance computing and artificial intelligence algorithms that dramatically shortened the process from several months to two weeks.
- The country used **emergency alert text messages** to millions of people using the Cellular Broadcasting Service, to inform the public of the whereabouts of confirmed patients, reinforce "social distancing," and to flag infection hotspots.
- **Data-driven epidemiological investigation was conducted** utilizing patient statements, credit card transaction logs, smartphone location tracking data, and CCTV footage for accurate tracing of transmission.
- A **self-diagnosis mobile application (app)** developed by the government allowed incoming travelers to monitor symptoms while also providing them prompt medical advice, while a **self-quarantine safety app** effectively supported the monitoring of those under self-quarantine—allowing users to monitor their conditions and conduct self-diagnosis, and sending alerts when they left quarantine areas. Installation of the mobile app was voluntary for those living in the ROK.

Source: Government of ROK. 2020. How Korea responded to a pandemic using ICT flattening the curve on COVID-19. 11 May.

the aftermath of the MERS outbreak enabled this detailed movement history to be made publicly available through government websites, text alerts, and mobile apps. While time-intensive and, at times, imperfect—for example, privacy concerns were also raised around making private data publicly available for fear of stigmatization—meticulous tracking and digital contract tracing has been very effective in identifying and isolating confirmed and suspected cases to prevent further disease transmission. Close contacts of confirmed and suspected cases, and those with recent travel to outbreak areas, were quarantined for 14 days (sometimes more) or until clear of infection. Quarantine was free for those in public centers. The ROK did not implement severe restrictive measures and, unlike most other countries, did not close borders, with the exception of a travel ban on passengers from Hubei, PRC. Additional containment measures therefore included mandatory screening for international arrivals at all ports of entry from 1 April 2020 and testing for symptomatic passengers and travelers. All international travelers were required to undergo a 14-day self-quarantine regardless of test results.

Early on, the government also prioritized nonpharmaceutical interventions to prevent the spread of COVID-19. Starting in January, the public was encouraged to wear masks and nonessential gatherings were discouraged to promote social-distancing. The government also closed schools and high-risk venues, encouraged online classes, and promoted virtual work systems. Between January and May, social-distancing restrictions were either made stricter or were relaxed depending on the case count. In June 2020, the country instituted a three-tiered system of social-distancing restrictions ranging from Level 1 when cases were manageable by the health system to Level 3, which prohibited gatherings of 10 people or more when daily infections exceeded 100. Twice-daily briefings conducted by the KCDC were used to keep the public informed of key information and updates.

Screening, triage, and separate facilities for people with and without COVID-19 symptoms reduced the risk of spreading the virus within facilities. By the end of April, more than half of a million tests were conducted throughout the country. On 30 April, the country reported just four cases, all of them imported from travelers.[32] This marked the first day with zero local infections since the first case was identified in January.

Treatment

At the start of the outbreak, the government hospitalized all patients who tested positive for COVID-19. However, a surge in cases quickly overloaded health system capacity, resulting in bed shortages for critical patients. In response, the government established a patient management system to diagnose COVID-19 patients based on their symptoms (footnote 6). Patient flow was managed by a national-level coordination center, with the new protocols applied throughout the country (footnote 19). By June, the government had significantly increased health system capacity through a triage system that separated treatment procedures according to patient severity and by scaling isolation units and screening centers throughout the country.[33] Telehealth services were also adopted to contain the virus spread in hospitals and clinics and among healthcare workers. All in-hospital care and treatment costs for confirmed patients are covered free of charge.

Risk communication and community engagement

Following criticism for withholding critical information during the MERS outbreak, from very early in the COVID-19 outbreak, the Government of the ROK prioritized transparent, consistent, and timely communication with the public across several platforms. These included twice-a-day press briefings from the KCDC, national social-distancing, and infectious disease alert levels and messages

[32]   A. Sternlicht. 2020. South Korea's Widespread Testing and Contact Tracing Lead to First Day With No New Cases. *Forbes*. 30 April. https://www.forbes.com/sites/alexandrasternlicht/2020/04/30/south-koreas-widespread-testing-and-contact-tracing-lead-to-first-day-with-no-new-cases/?sh=36bacc4f5abf

[33]   Ariadne Labs. 2020. *Global Learnings Evidence Brief: Protecting Health Care Workers in South Korea During the COVID-19 Pandemic*. Boston. https://covid19.ariadnelabs.org/wp-content/uploads/sites/6/2020/05/Ariadne-Labs-Global-Learnings-Evidence-Brief-Protecting-Health-Care-Workers-in-South-Korea.pdf.

through text alerts, websites, mobile apps, and posters. For example, the country used its public warning system to send out emergency alerts that provided status updates and other anonymous details of confirmed cases simultaneously to millions of mobile users.[34] In addition, the country's Ministry of Foreign Affairs created a public diplomacy campaign, the TRUST campaign—an acronym for "Transparency, Robust screening and quarantine, Unique but universally applicable testing, Strict control, and Treatment"[35]—which outlined the government's five-pillared response. To reinforce these messages, a coordinated public health information campaign was rolled out.

Financing

The COVID-19 response has largely been financed through the NHI.[36] In order to address the economic impact of COVID-19, in March 2020, parliament approved a W11.7 trillion ($9 billion) package for COVID-19 response to cover costs related to the healthcare crisis and to provide assistance to small- and medium-sized enterprises. An additional W12.2 trillion ($10 billion) was approved in April, with an additional W35.1 trillion ($29 billion) approved in July to provide financial support for companies and to expand employment support, social safety nets, and disease control.[37] Specific measures included income tax breaks for landlords, value-added tax breaks for small businesses, loans to the country's biggest airlines, employment support for hard-hit sectors like tourism, and stimulus checks to citizens. The Bank of Korea also took steps to support the economy, including cutting rates and establishing a $60 billion bilateral reciprocal credit line with the US Federal Reserve.[38] However, while the economy has continued to shed jobs and many sectors have been hard hit—including the services, travel, lodging and

food, and wholesale and retail sectors—exports of medical supplies and pharmaceuticals, test kits, hand sanitizers, and antibiotics have increased. Still, recent data indicate that COVID-19 has pushed the ROK into a recession, with the sharpest decline in GDP since 1998.[39]

Leadership

Decisive leadership, early action, and a strong chain of command have driven the country's response to COVID-19. The country took immediate steps in the initial stages of the outbreak to activate emergency response protocols, ensuring a whole-of-government approach. This included engaging the private sector in the rapid development of test kits; raising national alerts quickly; working across government departments to activate extensive testing, tracing, and tracking; providing free masks through community centers; authorizing the flexible relocation of resources; and a willingness to adopt innovations (i.e., drive-through testing). Also, when engaging in risk communication about the virus, the country's political leadership placed scientific experts at the forefront of efforts to deliver clear, unambiguous advice, with the KCDC director leading the country's twice-daily briefings. Within this framework, the country was able to deliver a cohesive, clear, and rational case to the public on the most effective measures to stop the chain of virus transmission. Finally, the country embraced regional and international cooperation through the exportation of medical supplies and transparent sharing of best practices, lessons learned, and clinical data.

Cross-sector Cooperation

Cross-sector cooperation proved vital in coordinating action, developing innovations, and engaging communities. Central and local governments worked closely together to address

---

[34] UNDP Seoul Policy Exchange. 2020. *Korea's Rapid Innovations in the Time of COVID-19*. Press release. UNDP. 23 March. https://www.undp.org/content/seoul_policy_center/en/home/presscenter/articles/2019/korea_s-rapid-innovations-in-the-time-of-covid-19.html.

[35] Government of the Republic of Korea. 2020. *TRUST Campaign to Fight against COVID-19 (8) Lessons Learned and the Way Forward*. 8 April. http://overseas.mofa.go.kr/ca-toronto-en/brd/m_5279/view.do?seq=760671.

[36] A. Salmon. 2020. Inside Korea's Low-cost, High-tech Covid-19 Strategy. *Asia Times*. 15 June. https://asiatimes.com/2020/06/the-secrets-behind-south-koreas-covid-19-success/.

[37] IMF. 2020. *Policy Responses to COVID-19*. 27 August. IMF. https://www.imf.org/en/Topics/imf-and-covid19/Policy-Responses-to-COVID-19.

[38] T. Stangarone. 2020. Building South Korea's economy after the great pandemic recession. *East Asia Forum*. 29 July. https://www.eastasiaforum.org/2020/07/29/building-south-koreas-economy-after-the-great-pandemic-recession/.

[39] BBC. 2020. Coronavirus: South Korea Falls into Recession as Exports Slump. 23 July. https://www.bbc.com/news/business-53496522.

bed shortages, institute patient triage systems, and allocate resources (both financial and human). Furthermore, a whole-of-government approach was adopted and included action across a number of ministries—including the Ministry of the Interior and Safety, which oversees the National Disaster and Safety Control Center, along with emergency preparedness, response, and recovery (footnote 10); the Ministry of Economy and Finance, which approved economic stimulus measures; and the Ministry of the Interior and Safety, which worked with other government agencies, mobile network providers, and other private companies to send out the emergency alert messages.[40] Notably, the Government of the ROK also established robust public–private partnerships. This included close collaboration in several areas, including test kit development, utilization of private hospitals and laboratory facilities (the vast majority of which were in the private sector), manufacturing of masks and medical supplies, the repurposing of residential buildings owned by large private companies into treatment centers,[41] and the development of dashboards to increase public awareness and apps to track an individual's proximity to confirmed cases. Civil society also played a significant role by providing disaster relief, raising awareness, and reaching vulnerable groups.

Best Practices and Lessons Learned

Investing in preparedness

Existing health system capacity and preparedness gave the ROK an edge in managing COVID-19 effectively. The ROK's existing public health infrastructure and capacity, along with recent investments to bolster its pandemic response systems, paved the way for its COVID-19 response. Recent outbreaks prompted the government

to reassess its preparedness for public health emergencies and further reinforce the resilience of its health system. Specifically, after the country's experience with MERS, the government made a concerted effort to strengthen their capabilities and systems for public health emergency response—allocating more funding to the KCDC, strengthening surveillance systems, increasing the number of professional epidemiological investigators, improving hospital infection prevention and control, improving diagnostic testing capabilities by enlisting the private sector, and revising public health legislature to fast-track authorizations and enable meticulous contact tracing. At the same time, prior investments in digital health data infrastructure and data analytics proved invaluable in guiding decision making. As a result of these public health investments, the country was in many ways well-placed to respond to a public health emergency like COVID-19 before it occurred.

Executing clearsighted strategies with agility

The government's clear strategy helped to focus its response and resources, while its agile and adaptive leadership enabled rapid implementation of key innovations. Early on, the ROK made the simple decision to test and trace as many people as possible. The government's rapid but clearsighted leadership enabled the country to then maximize its existing capacity and investments. Once this strategic focus was laid out, it was enhanced through a number of innovations such as the rapid development of test kits, drive-through testing facilities, and a restructuring of triage and treatment. Since being piloted in February, the drive- and walk-through testing models were established across the country and have been adopted by many others.

In response to an outbreak of cases in the Daegu region, including a severe shortage of intensive care unit beds for severe and critically-ill patients, local

40   UNDP Seoul Policy Centre for Knowledge Exchange through SDG Partnerships. 2020. *Korea's Rapid Innovations in the Time of COVID-19.* 23 March. https://www.undp.org/content/seoul_policy_center/en/home/presscenter/articles/2019/korea_s-rapid-innovations-in-the-time-of-covid-19.html.

41   D. Yoon. 2020. How South Korea Solved Its Acute Hospital-Bed Shortage. *Wall Street Journal.* 22 March. https://www.wsj.com/articles/how-south-korea-solved-its-acute-hospital-bed-shortage-11584874801.

health officials and the government quickly changed course and reorganized the health system through a robust triage system to maximize efficiencies and reduce spread of the disease. This included securing community treatment centers for patients with mild illness to relieve hospital bed shortages and establishing special non-COVID-19 hospitals to ensure safety of non-COVID-19 patients (footnote 33). The country also applied digital solutions to gain intelligence on the spread of the epidemic and to suppress the resurgence of local outbreaks without major disruptions.

Furthermore, throughout initial stages of the outbreak, when the public was most likely to panic, the government remained engaged. Centralized leadership and coordination with active cooperation across subnational levels of government, helped to facilitate the government's agile and adaptive response.

Harnessing data and technology

Integration of data and digital innovation into existing public health-care systems significantly boosted the ROK's pandemic response. Building on its dynamic digital infrastructure and ICT sector—along with revised legislation following MERS that allowed for real-time tracing—authorities swiftly deployed digital tools and solutions to contain COVID-19. This included the use of big data and artificial intelligence that enabled fast testing; the use of location, surveillance and transaction data; self-diagnosis apps to monitor symptoms; and apps to provide real-time data on the locations of COVID-19 positive individuals (footnote 28).

In a country where an estimated 95% of adults own a smart phone,[42] using mobile technology to track patients and communicate public health messages was an effective way to harness its full potential. Furthermore, the government had wide public support for cell phone tracking and the use of anonymized personal data as long as confirmed patients' identities were not revealed. General opinion indicated that this published information allowed for better decision making. Research from the University of Chicago revealed that public disclosure of data shifted people's social activities and their commuting routes away from areas with higher infection rates.[43]

The use of digital data proved vital in determining where infections were higher and therefore where public health efforts could be directed. While public opinion has largely favored this level of surveillance—and in fact it was public demand that led to the legal revisions that allowed disclosure of details of confirmed cases—concerns about data privacy violations and social stigmatization have been raised.[44] In response, the country's National Human Rights Commission called for stronger measures to protect identities and the KCDC issued updates on disclosure to surveillance guidelines.[45]

Discussion

While the case of the ROK sheds important light on which discrete measures worked within their context and were more effective than others (e.g., testing to cut the chain of infection, strategic use of data and digital solutions, clearsighted leadership, and early action), it also offers insight into two other equally important aspects of their response. First, many of these actions were interrelated and were quickly and simultaneously taken.[46] Second, and perhaps more importantly, the

42 J. Fendos. 2020. How Surveillance Technology Powered South Korea's COVID-19 Response. *Brookings Institute.* 29 April. https://www.brookings.edu/techstream/how-surveillance-technology-powered-south-koreas-covid-19-response/.

43 D. Argente, C.-T. Hsieh, and M. Lee. 2020. The Cost of Privacy: Welfare Effects of the Disclosure of COVID-19 Cases. *Becker Friedman Institute for Economics at UChicago Working Paper.* No. 2020-64. https://bfi.uchicago.edu/wp-content/uploads/BFI_WP_202064.pdf.

44 S.-Y. Oh. 2020. South Korea's Success Against COVID-19. *The Regulatory Review.* 15 May. https://www.theregreview.org/2020/05/14/oh-south-korea-success-against-covid-19/.

45 M. S. Kim. 2020. Seoul's Radical Experiment in Digital Contact Tracing. *The New Yorker.* 17 April. https://www.newyorker.com/news/news-desk/seouls-radical-experiment-in-digital-contact-tracing.

46 G. Pisano, R. Sadun, and M. Zanini. 2020. Lessons from Italy's Response to Coronavirus. *Harvard Business Review.* 27 March. https://hbr.org/2020/03/lessons-from-italys-response-to-coronavirus.

ROK's response to COVID-19 was deeply informed by its past experience and its present model of healthcare—which emphasizes equitable access through UHC. In other words, the country's response reflects systematic and deliberate investments across discrete parts of the healthcare system (e.g., testing facilities, hospitals, and health data) and between the public and private sector over time.

The ROK's success in testing provides a good example of both of these points. Coupled with decisive action, the country's testing strategy was amplified by its ability to activate diagnostic capacity and digital innovation simultaneously. It also reflected the country's bureaucratic agility—a capacity for government agencies to move quickly and coordinate action centrally. At the same time, the country's testing capacity was the result of years of investment in complex health infrastructure, including laboratory hardware and technicians, logistics, and information technology.[47]

Furthermore, the country has been striving to ensure that all people and communities receive quality health services and are protected from health threats. This includes not only recent efforts to establish coordinated whole-of-government pandemic response mechanisms at all levels but several reforms to improve efficiency and equity in access to healthcare through UHC.

Although the country has had challenges in its delivery of healthcare—including a fragmented and privatized delivery system, and high OOP payments that have placed a heavy burden on households, especially the most vulnerable—it has prioritized investments in its health infrastructure. As a result of lessons learned, it has also created an enabling environment through policies and legislation that have allowed authorities to take the necessary steps to actually respond to emergency public health needs immediately. In this way, pandemic preparedness has been recognized as a core public health function, with the requisite investments in the core capabilities required to deliver a robust response.

Conclusion

Making decisions in a crisis is inherently challenging, even when a country has the benefit of a head start, like the ROK. Indeed, the country experienced a second spike in cases in May, and a third in August, which spread throughout the country, raising concerns about bed shortages and prompting the government to tighten restrictions. A fourth spike starting in November has demonstrated just how difficult the virus is to contain, even for countries who appear to have controlled it. Fortunately, by international standards, the country's case count and total number of deaths remains enviably low, suggesting that the country's strategies do appear to have some measure of durability.

While questions remain about the country's ability to conduct such time and resource-intensive efforts—especially as the November outbreak appeared to have spread quietly through community transmission—overall, the case of the ROK demonstrates how long-term investments in and prioritization of public health systems, including UHC, combined with clear leadership and public trust can coalesce to create an effective national strategy. However, what underpins the country's response actions is not only that they reflected the strategic importance of strengthening health systems, but also that they were activated quickly and simultaneously. This was largely possible due to systematic and deliberate investments across the health system (e.g., diagnostics, infection control, and health data) and between public and private sectors.

The ROK's experience also highlights how errors and missteps from one pandemic can be turned into actionable lessons learned for the next. Hopefully, these same investments and lessons can support the complex rollout of a coronavirus vaccine in the coming months. Thus, as the pandemic continues to unfold, the ROK's strategies—although specific to their context—can, it is hoped, shed light on the vital role investments in public health systems play in safeguarding health and economic security.

---

47   C. Hankla. 2020. Why Some Countries Have Responded More Effectively to COVID-19 Than Others. *Yes Magazine.* 15 May. https://www.yesmagazine.org/democracy/2020/05/15/coronavirus-countries-success/.

2   Thailand

Executive Summary

Confirmation of the coronavirus disease (COVID-19) pandemic was announced in Thailand on 13 January 2020, when the country reported the first case of the virus outside the People's Republic of China (PRC). The first reported locally transmitted case occurred on 31 January. From January to March, the case count increased gradually, then quickly rose to over 3,000 cases, until plateauing from May onward. Through extensive measures, including early response and partial lockdown, Thailand was able to contain the spread of COVID-19. Equipped with field epidemiology training programs and laboratory systems, the Ministry of Public Health (MOPH) as the core agency, with support from the Department of Disease Control, Department of Medical Services, and the Bamrasnaradura Infectious Diseases Institute, continues a proactive approach to monitoring and tracking the disease. As of 1 November 2020, the country had 3,784 confirmed cases.[1]

Thailand has received global recognition for its successful introduction and adoption of universal healthcare (UHC) in 2002 through three public health insurance schemes: the Civil Servant Medical Benefit Scheme (CSMBS), the Social Health Insurance (SHI), and the Universal Coverage Scheme (UCS). The UCS—covering close to 75% of the entire population with favorable pro-poor outcomes—is funded through a general tax and managed by the National Health Security Office (NHSO). Prior to COVID-19, Thailand's healthcare and health security capacities were recognized by the Global Health Security Index (GHSI) 2019.[2]

Across 195 countries, Thailand has the sixth highest overall score (73.2, with global average of 40.2). It ranked second for a robust health system (70.5, average 26.4) and third in disease prevention (75.7, average 34.8). Based on the Joint External Evaluation (JEE) of the World Health Organization (WHO) in 2017, Thailand established a strong capacity to implement the International Health Regulations (IHR), including national legislation and policy response, field epidemiology training programs, real-time surveillance, and risk communication.[3]

Key lessons learned

Investment in the health system and UHC. Thailand has made significant investments in public health over the past 40 years. Most importantly, the extension of rural health services nationwide has increased access to healthcare at community levels. This includes more than 10,000 primary healthcare (PHC) facilities and more than 1,000 public hospitals offering secondary and tertiary care services, with approximately 12,500 beds at field hospitals nationwide. Health personnel and established networks—notably provincial health offices, hospitals and health centers, and frontline village health volunteers (VHVs)—have been able to support active-case finding, disease surveillance, and effectively reach out to people within the community. As a result of these accessible health

---

1   Ministry of Public Health, Thailand. 2020. *The Coronavirus Disease 2019 Thailand Situation Update on 1 November 2020*. Nonthaburi.

2   Nuclear Threat Initiative. 2019. *Global Health Security Index: Bringing Collective Action and Accountability*. ghsindex.org/wp-content/uploads/2020/04/2019-Global-Health-Security-Index.pdf.

3   WHO. 2017. *Joint External Evaluation of IHR Core Capacities of the Kingdom of Thailand, Mission Report*. Geneva.

facilities and community outreach programs, Thailand has been able to monitor the spread of COVID-19 and avoid major outbreaks.

Early response. From the onset, starting with the country's first case of COVID-19 in January 2020, Thailand's MOPH has shown strong leadership through coordinated efforts from various departments, including deploying existing field laboratories that have been crucial in making important, evidence-based decisions. The MOPH Department of Disease Control initiated screening measures at points of entry and prepared the department's workforce in responding to potential outbreaks. In addition, the Department of Medical Sciences has set standards and ensures the quality of laboratory testing. Bans on international travel and partial lockdowns have also helped contain COVID-19 outbreaks in Thailand.

A holistic government approach and strong public compliance. Establishing the Centre for COVID-19 Situation Administration (CCSA) provided a focal point of response to COVID-19 and effective regular communication with the public. The Department of Disease Control provides daily status reports and coordinates essential health information. Strong public compliance with government mandatory measures such as curfews and restricted nonessential travel, as well as voluntary preventative measures (e.g., mask wearing, social distancing, and stay-at-home home orders) also played important roles in curbing any wide spread of COVID-19.

The impacts of COVID-19 are unprecedented. Not only have they stretched health system responses, but they have also exposed vulnerabilities in the economy and society. Thailand's health system is experiencing challenges, such as large regional inequalities and gaps in services for vulnerable populations like migrants. Thailand will continue to provide surveillance and aim to combat COVID-19 with resilience as it moves forward. While monitoring the health of its citizens and associated COVID-19 impacts, the country should also take into account the mental health outcomes associated with stress and isolation.

Moreover, post COVID-19 recovery will require new holistic visions and strategies to aid employment—

especially in the tourism, service, trade, and agriculture sectors, as well as local businesses. Finally, this Thailand case study demonstrates the importance of health systems and the benefits gained from health security preparedness, a strong foundation of PHC, and investment in UHC. Experiences from previous decades of development in the country's own health systems and lessons learned from other countries in the Asia and Pacific region could contribute to efforts to contain the current COVID-19 pandemic, and other future emerging infectious diseases, and mitigate its negative impacts.

Introduction

The COVID-19 pandemic was officially announced in Thailand on 13 January 2020, when the country reported the first case of the virus outside the PRC. The first reported locally transmitted case occurred on 31 January. From January to March, the case count increased gradually, then quickly rose to over 3,000 cases, until plateauing from May onward. Through extensive measures, including early response and partial lockdown, Thailand has been able to mitigate the spread of COVID-19. Equipped with field epidemiology training programs and laboratory systems, the MOPH as the core agency, with support from the Department of Disease Control, Department of Medical Services, and the Bamrasnaradura Infectious Diseases Institute, continues a proactive approach to monitoring and tracking the disease. As of 1 November 2020, the country had 3,784 confirmed cases (footnote 1).

Background

Country context

The Kingdom of Thailand is situated in Southeast Asia, bordered by Cambodia, the Lao People's Democratic Republic, Malaysia, and Myanmar. Thailand is composed of 76 provinces, and has a population of over 69.8 million with half residing in urban areas (Table 2.1). Thailand's capital city, Bangkok ("Krung Thep"), is the most populous city hosting over eight million of the country's population. As of 2018, Thailand's administrative sector consists of central government, 76 provincial administrative organizations, 878 districts, and 2,442 municipalities. Following the 1999 Decentralisation Act, the country has moved toward transferring resources and authority from central to local governments (e.g., allocating over 25% of government revenue).

An upper middle-income country,[4] Thailand is ranked in the top five of the largest economies in Southeast Asia. Traditionally, the workforce has been heavily based on the agriculture sector. However, the manufacturing industries (e.g., automobiles, computers, and rubber), along with the service sector, now contribute over 40% of gross domestic product (GDP), with less than 15% from the agriculture sector. Despite an official report of 10% of the population living below the national poverty line and unemployment rates estimated at less than 1% in 2019,[5] income inequality has improved over the years but the Gini index has held steady at 36–41 since 2015 (Table 2.1). Thailand's GDP growth has been stable, averaging 2%–4% during 2013–2019.

Key health indicators and UHC

In the past few decades, Thailand has undergone a number of demographic and epidemiological shifts, with the transition to low fertility (currently at 1.5) and a decline and changing pattern of mortality (Table 2.1). As of 2018, life expectancy is 73 years for males and 80 years for females, with close to 20% of the population aged 60 years and older.[6] Since the late 1980s, noncommunicable diseases (NCDs) have emerged in the top five causes of death[7] and, as of 2017, 73.7% of causes of death can be attributed to NCDs according to the Global Burden of Disease 2017 (Table 2.1).

As of 2019, Thailand is on track to achieve the 2030 United Nations Sustainable Development Goal (SDG) #3 in ensuring healthy lives and promoting wellbeing for all. For example,[8] the country has achieved maternal mortality at 20 per 100,000 live births and under-five mortality at 9.5 per 1,000 live births (SDG targets 3.1 and 3.2), essential vaccines, diphtheria–tetanus–pertussis/DTP3 and measles-containing vaccine/MCV2 immunization coverage above 95%, and communicable diseases such as tuberculosis incidence rates as low as 156 per 100,000 population (SDG target 3.3).[9]

Thailand has received global recognition for successfully implementing UHC in 2002. Achievement of UHC is a core element of the SDG target 3.8.1 on access to essential health services and SDG target 3.8.2 on catastrophic expenditure on health. Thailand reports a UHC service coverage index of 79.8 (regional average for Southeast Asia of 55 on SDG target 3.8.1) and 2.2% of households experience catastrophic health expenditure at the 10% of total household expenditure compared to regional estimates of 12.8% (SDG target 3.8.2) (footnote 8).[10] Since adoption of UHC, out-of-pocket expenditure has declined substantially from 34% in 2001 to 14.8% in 2007 and 11.1% in 2017 (Table 2.1). Total health expenditure as a proportion of GDP has increased from 3.0% in 2001 to 3.7% by 2017. Domestic government health expenditure constitutes 15.3% of general government expenditure, significantly higher compared to regional estimates of 6.7% (footnote 8).

Thailand[11] continues to monitor three UHC dimensions: population coverage, service coverage (preventative and curative benefit packages), and financial risk protection.[12]

---

[4]   Based on per capita Gross National Income (GNI) of US$6,610, see Table 2.1.
[5]   ADB. 2020. Basic Statistics, April 2020. data.adb.org/dataset/basic-statistics-asia-and-pacific.
[6]   United Nations Population Division. 2019. *World Population Prospects 2019*. New York: UN.
[7]   V. Kosulwat. 2002. The Nutrition and Health Transition in Thailand. *Public Health and Nutrition*. 5 (1A). pp. 183–189.
[8]   WHO. 2019. *World Health Statistics 2019: Monitoring Health for the Sustainable Development Goals*. Geneva.
[9]   United Nations. 2020. *The Sustainable Development Goals Report 2020*. New York.
[10] WHO. 2019. *Primary Health Care on the Road to Universal Health Coverage 2019 Monitoring Report Conference Edition*. Geneva.
[11] W. Witthayapipopsakul et al. 2019. Achieving the Targets for Universal Health Coverage: How is Thailand Monitoring Progress? *WHO South East Asia Journal of Public Health*. 8 (1). pp. 10–17.
[12] V. Tangcharoensathien et al. 2018. Health Systems Development in Thailand: A Solid Platform for Successful Implementation of Universal Health Coverage. *Lancet*. 391 (10126). pp. 1205–1223.

Table 2.1: Thailand Country Context and Health System Indicators

	Indicators		Values
DEMOGRAPHIC AND ECONOMIC	Total population (in thousands) 2020[a]		69,800
	Population density (people per square meters of land area) 2018[b]		135.9
	Urban population (%) 2019[a]		50.7
	Urban population growth (annual %) 2019[a]		1.8
	GNI per capita, Atlas method (current $US) 2018[c]		6,610 (upper middle-income)
	Gini index (World Bank estimate) 2016–2018[c]		36.4
	GDP growth (annual %) 2020 forecast[d]		−6.5
	GDP growth (annual %) 2019[d]		2.4
	GDP growth (annual %) 2018[d]		4.2
	Labor force participation rate (% of 15–64 years) 2018[e]		74.6
	Labor force, female (% of total labor force) 2018[e]		45.6
	Literacy rate, adult total (% of 15 years+) 2018[f]		93.7
	Proportion, female (% of total population) 2019[a]		51.3
	Fertility rate (births per woman) 2018[a]		1.5
	Population ages 0–14 (% of total population) 2019[a]		16.8
	Life expectancy at birth, male (years) 2018[a]		73.2
	Life expectancy at birth, female (years) 2018[a]		80.7
	Population aged 60+ years (%) 2020[a]		19.2
	Population aged 60+ years (%) 2035[a]		30.5
	Population aged 75+ years (%) 2035[a]		10.0
HEALTH SYSTEM INDICATORS	**Causes of deaths, Global Burden of Diseases 2017[g]**		
	Communicable and maternal and child-related conditions		16.0%
	Noncommunicable diseases		73.7%
	Injuries		10.3%
	Current health expenditure (% GDP)[h]	2017	3.7
		2001	3.3
	Government expenditure on health (% of total government expenditure)[h]	2014	13.3
		2000	10.0
	Out-of-pocket expenditure (% of total health expenditure)[h]	2017	11.1
		2000	34.2
	Hospital beds (per 1,000 population)[i] 2010–2015		2.1
	Doctors (per 10,000 population)[i] 2016–2017		8.1
	Nurse and midwives (per 10,000 population)[i] 2015–2017		29.6
	Skilled health professional density (per 10,000 population)[i] 2012–2015		22.5
	Global Health Security Index (average score across 195 countries)[j]		
	Overall score (normalized scale of 0 to 100, where 100 = best health security)		73.2 (sixth of 195 countries)
	Prevention of the emergence of release pathogens (34.8)		75.7
	Detection and reporting for epidemic of potential international concern (41.9)		81.0
	Rapid response to mitigate of the spread of an epidemic (38.4)		78.6
	Health system to treat the sick and protect health workers (26.4)		70.5

GDP = gross domestic product, Gini = a measure of the distribution of income across a population, GNI = gross national income.

Sources:

[a] United Nations, Department of Economic and Social Affairs, Population Division. 2019. World Population Prospects 2019, custom data acquired via website.

[b] Food and Agriculture Organization and World Bank estimates.

[c] World Bank Open Data, World Development Indicators (data.worldbank.org)—calculated using the World Bank Atlas method, lower middle-income economies are those with a GNI per capita of $1,026–$3,995 and upper middle-income economies are those with a GNI per capita of $3,996–$12,375.

[d] ADB (adb.org/countries/thailand).

[e] International Labour Organization, ILOSTAT database, September 2019.

[f] UNESCO Institute for Statistics (uis.unesco.org/). United Nations Population Division. World Urbanization Prospects: 2018 Revision.

[g] Global Burden of Diseases 2017, data visualization (vizhub.healthdata.org/gbd-compare).

[h] WHO Global Health Expenditure database (https://apps.who.int/nha/database).

[i] Global Health Observatory, WHO (who.int/data/gho).

[j] Global Health Security Index: Bringing Collective Action and Accountability (ghsindex.org/wp-content/uploads/2020/04/2019-Global-Health-Security-Index.pdf).

Currently, Thais receive coverage through three public health insurance schemes:

- UHC, which covers approximately 72% of the population, is funded through general tax and managed by the NHSO. The NHSO manages payments based on a capitation basis (e.g., numbers of registered UHC members in service areas) for outpatient care, and diagnosis-related group-based payments with global budget for inpatient care.
- The CSMBS (9%) includes government employees and their beneficiaries. This noncontributory scheme is funded through the general tax under the Comptroller General Department of the Ministry of Finance.
- The SHI scheme (16%), which covers employees working in the private sector, excluding dependants. Contributions are shared equally by employer, employee, and the government and the scheme is managed through the Social Security Office of the Ministry of Labor.

Private insurance constitutes about 3% of the remaining population, including foreigners.

Health infrastructure, workforce, and PHC

Successful implementation of UHC in the country, including achieving good health at a low cost, can be attributed in part to comprehensive geographical coverage of PHC, with 9,761 health centers ("Tumbol subdistrict health promoting hospitals" โรงพยาบาลส่งเสริมสุขภาพตำบล) serving as gatekeepers and offering both preventative and curative health services. The PHC has contributed significantly to the scaling up of immunization coverage for children and also for regular monitoring of risk factors for NCDs[13] in the community.[14] After the PHC initial screening, UHC members are referred up the system for access to and use of specialized services. Secondary and tertiary care is provided by 34 regional hospitals, 84 provincial hospitals, and 781 district hospitals.[15]

Even before implementation of UHC, Thailand had invested not only in healthcare infrastructure but also human resources for health (footnote 12).[16] Thailand is fortunate to have a skilled healthcare workforce with a population density of medical doctors at 8.1 per 10,000 and a population density of nursing and midwifery personnel at 29.6 per 10,000 compared to regional averages of 7.4 and 19.9, respectively.[17] One distinctive contributor to the Thai health system since the 1970s is the VHVs "อาสาสมัครสาธารณสุข" that work in every village nationwide.[18] Despite the term "volunteers," each VHV receives B1,000 (about $32) per month. Today, over one million VHVs have been instrumental in delivering COVID-19 health information to communities and assessing and following up on symptoms. The VHVs have been invaluable in promoting trust in the Thai public health system.

Public health emergency experience

Across 195 countries, Thailand was the only middle-income country to score in the highest tier of the GHSI, an assessment of global health security capabilities (Table 2.1). The country was also ranked sixth for its overall score (73.2, global average 40.2), second for a robust health system (70.5, average 26.4), and third in disease prevention (75.7, average 34.8).

Based on WHO's JEE mission in 2017, Thailand has demonstrated success in implementing IHR, in particular national legislation and policy response (score 5 out of 5), field epidemiology training programs

---

13   V. Yiengprugsawan, J. Healy, and H. Kendig. 2016. *Health System Responses to Population Ageing and Noncommunicable Diseases in Asia.* WHO Regional Office for South-East Asia, Delhi: Asia Pacific Observatory on Health Systems and Policies.

14   K. Sumriddetchkajorn, K. Shimazaki, T. Ono, T. Kusaba, K. Sato, and N. Kobayashi. 2019. Universal Health Coverage and Primary Care, Thailand. *Bulletin WHO.* 97 (6) pp. 415–422.

15   P. Jongudomsuk et al. 2015. The Kingdom of Thailand Health System Review. In *Health Systems in Transition 5 (5).* WHO on behalf of the Asia Pacific Observatory on Health Systems and Policies.

16   S. Nitayarumphong, S. 1999. Evolution of Primary Health Care in Thailand: What Policies Worked? *Health Policy and Planning.* 5 (3) pp. 246–254.

17   WHO. 2020. Global Health Observatory. https://www.who.int/data/gho (accessed day month year).

18   K. Chuengsatiansup, and P. Suksuth. 2007. Health Volunteers in the Context of Change: Potential and Developmental Strategies. *Journal of Health Systems Research* 1 (3–4). pp. 268–279.

(score 5), real-time surveillance (score 4), and risk communication (score 4) (footnote 3).

Thailand's capacity to identify and stop infectious diseases was demonstrated in regard to Middle East Respiratory Syndrome, which was reported on 18 June 2015 to WHO with the first confirmed case of a traveler from Oman to Bangkok. The country was able to contain the case with no further spread. This success—which included no secondary transmissions—was a result of a collaborative effort between the Ministries of Health in Oman and Thailand, both of whom followed IHR mechanisms including timely reports to the WHO.[19] The MOPH as the core agency, including the Department of Disease Control, has a robust system for monitoring and tracking diseases, along with field epidemiology training programs, and national and subnational laboratory systems. Other examples of the MOPH's successful infection control include the early containment of Severe Acute Respiratory Syndrome (SARS)[20] and the prevention of the avian influenza (H5N1 or bird flu) in the mid-2000s. For the latter, the VHVs[21] had an essential role in early warning, surveillance, and promoting preventative health behaviors.[22]

COVID-19 in Thailand

Overall transmission dynamic

COVID-19 was reported in Thailand on 13 January 2020, when the country verified a case that originated in the PRC. Local transmission was first confirmed on 31 January 2020 by the MOPH. This was the first reported case in the country with no record of travel to the PRC.[23] New cases increased rapidly in March, with more than 100 cases reported daily. The source of

many of these infections was presumed to have been boxing stadiums and entertainment venues.[24]

In late February, 2 weeks before the WHO declared COVID-19 a pandemic, Thailand had declared the disease dangerous and communicable under the Disease Control Act in order to intensify surveillance and containment efforts.[25] Following the declaration of a state of emergency on 26 March 2020 (Figure 2.1), a curfew was announced between 10 p.m. and 4 a.m., starting on 3 April. During the Bangkok partial lockdown from early April, only supermarkets, pharmacies, and takeaway restaurants were allowed to stay open at malls. Nonessential travel between provinces was discouraged. Starting on 3 April, international flights were suspended and varying degrees of lockdown were enforced throughout the country. Many provincial governors also acted quickly and temporarily closed provincial borders.

Since the very first case of COVID-19 in January, the Thai MOPH Department of Disease Control activated its Emergency Operations Centers to respond to potential outbreaks. The government accelerated the response at the national level through the CCSA. The CCSA served as a central command center, engaging the whole government to manage the pandemic comprehensively. As fewer cases and deaths were reported, the government eased restrictions. Shopping malls and restaurants, markets, and other public venues were allowed to reopen on 17 May 2020. As of 1 July, education institutions had resumed activities, with no new cases for more than 30 days, signifying the completion of the first wave of COVID-19. From the beginning of July to the end of September, there were approximately 350 new cases.[26]

19   T. Plipat et al. 2015. Imported case of Middle East Respiratory Syndrome Coronavirus (Mers-Cov) infection from Oman to Thailand, June 2015. *Euro Surveillance* 22 (33). 30598. doi: 10.2807/1560-7917.ES.2017.22.33.30598.

20   A. Chaovavanich et al. 2004. Early Containment of Severe Acute Respiratory Syndrome (SARS); experience from Bamrasnaradura Institute, Thailand. *Journal of the Medical Association of Thailand* 87. pp. 1182–1187.

21   WHO. 2007. *Role of Village Health Volunteers in Avian Influenza Surveillance in Thailand.* WHO, Regional Office for South-East Asia.

22   T. Silawan, and J. Petsuk. 2011. Preventive behaviors and roles of village health volunteers in prevention and control of avian influenza. *Journal of Health Education.* 19 (12). pp. 125–135.

23   W.A. Pongpirul et al. 2020. Journey of a Thai Taxi Driver and Novel Coronavirus. *New England Journal of Medicine.* 382 (11). pp. 1067–1068.

24   S. Sirilak. 2020. *Thailand's Experience in the Covid-19 Response.* Ministry of Public Health, Thailand.

25   WHO. 2020. *WHO Thailand Situation Report - 29 February 2020.* https://www.who.int/docs/default-source/searo/thailand/20200229-tha-sitrep-11-covid-19-final.pdf.

26   Ministry of Public Health of Thailand. 2020. Daily Situation Reports. https://ddc.moph.go.th/viralpneumonia/eng/situation.php.

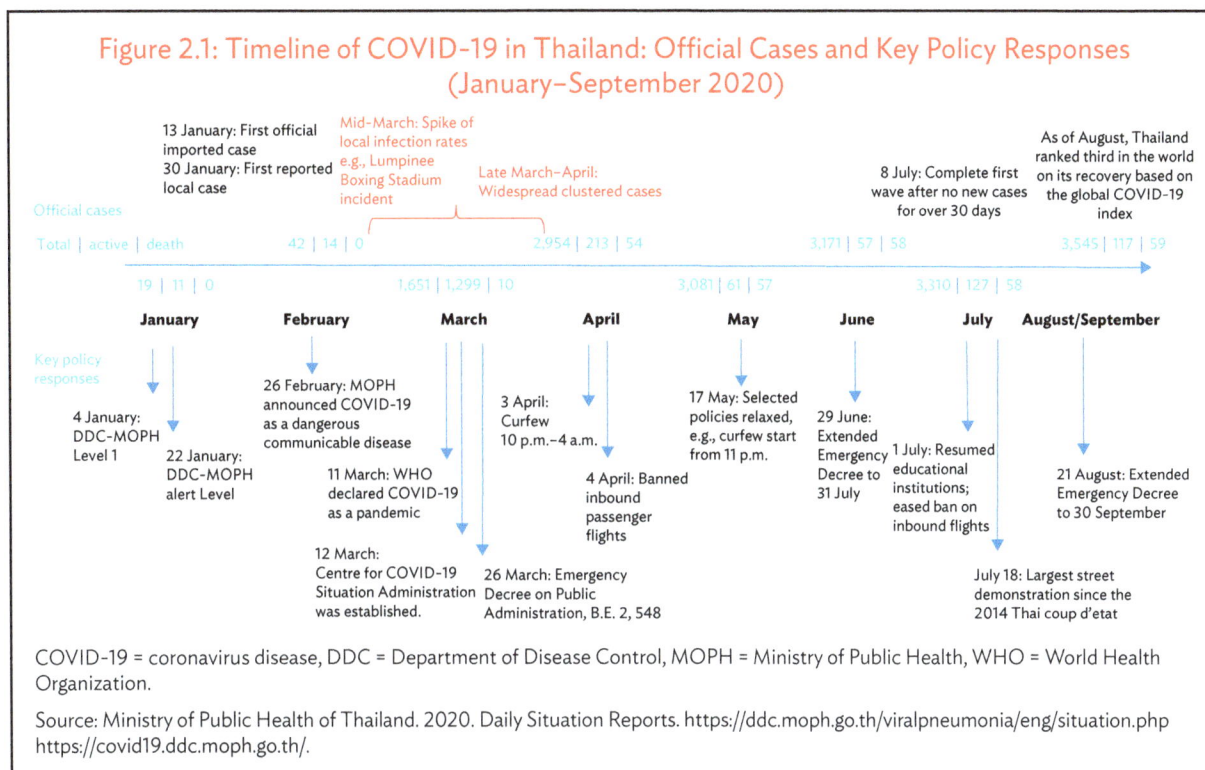

Figure 2.1: Timeline of COVID-19 in Thailand: Official Cases and Key Policy Responses (January–September 2020)

COVID-19 = coronavirus disease, DDC = Department of Disease Control, MOPH = Ministry of Public Health, WHO = World Health Organization.

Source: Ministry of Public Health of Thailand. 2020. Daily Situation Reports. https://ddc.moph.go.th/viralpneumonia/eng/situation.php https://covid19.ddc.moph.go.th/.

Detection

As of 1 November 2020, there were 918, 835 cases tested and 3,784 confirmed cases (2,451 local transmission and 1,333 imported cases), 122 undergoing treatment, and 59 deaths.[27]

- The median age of confirmed cases was 36 years, with 2,133 cases are men, and 1,651 cases are women.
- Among the total cases tested, over half received medical services on their own at hospitals (337,475 cases in public hospitals and 150, 427 cases in private hospitals).

Surveillance has been conducted at three different levels:

1. **points of entry**, including quarantine stations with body temperature ≥37.5°C or with respiratory symptoms including cough, running nose, or difficulty breathing;

2. **hospitals or healthcare facilities** and surveillance of health personnel; and

3. **community case finding**, conducted by provincial public health officials, VHVs, and other related public and private sector agencies.

According to the Department of Disease Control active-case finding guidelines,[28] suspected cases who were symptomatic were tested immediately. All suspected cases, whether symptomatic or asymptomatic, were quarantined for at least 14 days. In the case that sustained transmission of COVID-19 was reported after 28 days, surveillance was to be conducted for asymptomatic infections in identified areas (e.g., communities and villages). In collaboration, the Ministry of Digital Economy and Society and the Department of Disease Control developed the "Thai Chana" and "Mor Chana" web applications as a tracking and screening system to

---

[27] MOPH, Thailand. *The Coronavirus Disease 2019 Thailand Situation Update on 1 November 2020.* Nonthaburi: Department of Disease Control: Ministry of Public Health. https://ddc.moph.go.th/viralpneumonia/eng/file/situation/situation-no301-011163.pdf.

[28] MOPH, Thailand. 2020. *Guidelines for Surveillance and Investigation of Coronavirus Disease 2019 (COVID-19).* Version 15 May. Nonthaburi: Department of Disease Control: Ministry of Public Health. https://ddc.moph.go.th/viralpneumonia/eng/file/guidelines/g_surveillance_230620n.pdf.

Figure 2.2: "Thai Chana" and "Mor Chana" Application Platform

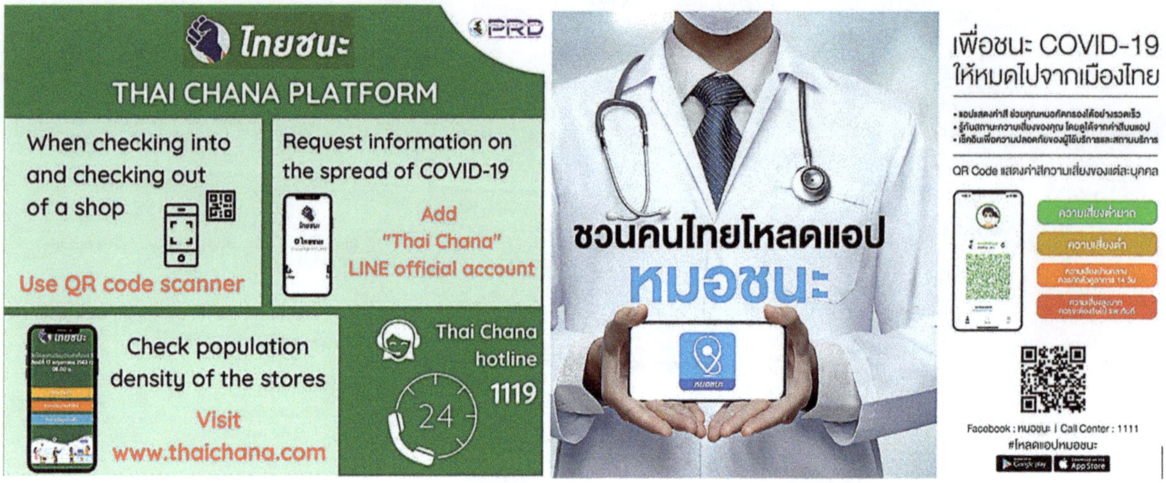

Sources: Government of Thailand. Centre for COVID-19 Situation Administration. 2020; and Cat Datacom. 2021. Applications Needed for Monitoring "Covid-19". News release. 21 January. https://www.cattelecom.com/cat/siteContent/4000/275/Applications+needed+for+monitoring+%22Covid+19%22+.

assess COVID-19 risks and assist health authorities in tracking population movement data (Figure 2.2).

Containment and treatment

The Department of Medical Services and the Department of Health Services Support were responsible for increasing the number of negative-pressure hospital rooms, managing hospital beds, and preparing field hospitals. Main services provided by public hospitals (80% public and 20% private) for COVID-19 treatment services along with private hospitals, and 12,537 beds were made available in field hospitals nationwide (footnote 24). All hospitals have to report cases to the MOPH (COVID-19 Clinical Management Oversight Committee, Department of Disease Control and Department of Medical Services).[29]

The Thai Food and Drug Administration procured personal protective equipment (PPE), including masks, ventilators, coveralls, disposable gloves, favipiravir, and other antiviral medicines for hospitals nationwide.

As of 8 July 2020, 205 COVID-19 laboratories were scaled up: 79 laboratories (35 government and 44 private labs) in Bangkok and 126 laboratories (102 government and 24 private labs) across the country (footnote 24). Regional laboratory centers provided back-up testing with a turnaround time of 24 hours. Different strategies were employed in locked-down districts (e.g., Phuket) such as drive-through testing or utilization of mobile teams where active contact tracing was put into place.[30] Collaboration between government and private sectors resulted in a rapid expansion of the COVID-19 laboratory network. Moreover, an integrated, national health database platform called "Co-Lab and Co-Ward," was used for data collection, diagnoses, treatment, and treatment reimbursement (footnote 24).

For confirmed cases, strict adherence to the COVID-19 guidelines issued by the Department of Medical Services, MOPH, on 13 March 2020 helped to streamline diagnosis and treatment. Cases were categorized into three groups: mild cases (only symptomatic treatment); mild cases in a high-risk

---

[29]   Department of Disease Control, Thai Ministry of Public Health. 2020. *Guidelines for clinical practice, diagnosis, treatment and prevention of healthcare-associated infection in response to patients with COVID-19 infection.* Version dated 8 April 2020, for Medical and Healthcare Personnel ddc.moph.go.th/viralpneumonia/eng/file/guidelines/g_CPG.pdf.

[30]   Asia Pacific Observatory on Health Systems and Policies. 2020. *COVID-19 health system response monitor, Thailand.* WHO. Regional Office for South-East Asia.

group (e.g., >60 years, chronic pulmonary disease, chronic kidney disease, heart failure, cirrhosis, and obesity)—two-drug combinations of chloroquine and lopinavir/ritonavir or darunavir/ritonavir for 5 days; and pneumonia cases—three-drug combinations of chloroquine, favipiravir, and lopinavir/ritonavir or darunavir/ritonavir for 10 days.[31] Patients received symptomatic and supportive care and the country's case fatality rate was less than 2% and lower than the global rate of over 4%.[32] Healthcare-related expenses of COVID-19 patients are covered by one of three public health insurance schemes: CSMBS, SHI, and UCS. Because there is no upfront cost or long waiting periods, many potential cases have been able to access testing and treatment in a timely manner.

Public communication and engagement

The CCSA and the MOPH designated Taweesin Visanuyothin—a CCSA spokesperson—to provide daily COVID-19 situational updates and information through live broadcasting. Effective communication from trusted sources has helped reduce anxiety among the Thai public and promote protective health behaviors.[33] Public cooperation has been adopted relatively well, including early adoption of face masks, the practice of "social distancing," and complying with "work-from-home" measures. During the partial lockdown, all department stores (except groceries) and businesses have adapted and offered services such as takeaway meals. Provincial and local governments are strictly monitoring organized public, cultural, and religious gatherings and other activities (i.e., gyms, barbershops, markets, restaurants, and sporting venues). The Songkran holiday, a major 5-day national holiday in April, was also postponed as part of Thailand's preventative measures.

Financing mechanisms and economic impacts

As a result of COVID-19, GDP of the Thai economy is forecast to contract by 6.5% in 2020 (GDP loss of $45 billion).[34] Thailand's tourism sector, one of the most significant contributors to GDP, has been severely affected since closing its international borders in April 2020. Domestically, nearly 21 million workers in Thailand were employed in sectors that are vulnerable, including retail, trade, and manufacturing. The National Economic and Social Development Council estimated that 8.4 million jobs are likely to be disrupted, including 2.5 million in the tourism sector, 4.4 million in other service sectors, and 1.5 million in the industry sector.[35]

The Ministry of Finance and the Bank of Thailand have also played crucial roles in mitigating medium- and long-term economic impacts and implementing revival plans. The Thai Cabinet approved three phases of a social, economic relief and stimulus package: Phase 1, totaling B207 million ($6.3 million); Phase 2 totaling B148 million ($4.5 million); and Phase 3 totaling B1.9 trillion ($58 billion), including cash assistance for farmers and workers affected by COVID-19 (e.g., B5,000 per month for farmers as well as nonfarm workers outside the SHI), a reduction in water and electricity bills, and a wide range of measures to support the country's tourism.[36] Domestic stimulus travel packages (totaling B22.4 billion or $720 million)[37] led by the Ministry of Finance and Ministry of Tourism and Sports, include a moral support subsidy for 1.2 million frontline medical personnel, health volunteers, and staff from subdistrict hospitals with B2,000 for 2 days and 1 night. For other Thais, the government also provides a subsidy package for up to B3,000 per night for 5 nights at participating hotels. The travel period related to the stimulus package was dated from July to October 2020. Multisectoral

[31] Department of Medical Services, Thai Ministry of Public Health. 2020. Treatment Guidelines for COVID-19. 13 March. https://ddc.moph.go.th/viralpneumonia/eng/file/guidelines/g_treatment.pdf.

[32] The Centre of Evidence-Based Medicine. 2020. Global Covid-19 Case Fatality Rates. https://www.cebm.net/covid-19/global-covid-19-case-fatality-rates/.

[33] R. Goodwin et al. 2020. Anxiety and Public Responses to COVID-19: Early Data from Thailand. *Journal of Psychiatric Research.* 129. pp. 118–121.

[34] ADB. 2020. *Asian Development Outlook Supplement: Lockdown, Loosening, and Asia's Growth Prospects.* Manila.

[35] ILO. 2020. *COVID-19 Employment and Labour Market Impact in Thailand,* June 2020.

[36] ADB. 2020. *Report and Recommendation of the President to the Board of Directors: Proposed Countercyclical Support Facility Loans Kingdom of Thailand: COVID-19 Active Response and Expenditure Support Program.* Manila.

[37] *TATnews,* Tourism Authority of Thailand. 2020. Thailand Approves Domestic Tourism Package Worth 22.4 Billion Baht. 17 June. tatnews.org/2020/06/thailand-approves-domestic-tourism-package-worth-22-4-billion-baht/.

support from different government and private agencies has helped to address not only health but also social and economic impacts.

Leadership and multisectoral cooperation

Government and sector leadership has contributed to the success of COVID-19 response in Thailand. Strong leadership led by Anutin Charnvirakul, Deputy Prime Minister and Minister of Public Health, as well as high-level administrators from the Department of Disease Control, Department of Medical Services, and Department of Health Service Support has enabled Thailand to respond efficiently to the pandemic. Furthermore, the Prime Minister declared a national state of emergency to facilitate the management of COVID-19 response in a comprehensive manner.

Managing the return of Thai citizens from overseas has required multisectoral cooperation. For example, the Ministry of Foreign Affairs (MOFA) was the main coordinator in bringing Thais back home, and an online platform was established to register Thais intending to return home. However, there have been some challenges, including Thais returning from high-risk areas such as Wuhan (PRC) during the early outbreak and undocumented Thai workers returning from the Republic of Korea.[38] Several agencies such as the MFA, MOPH, and the Ministries of Defence and Interior, and including hotel operators, are overseeing and coordinating a massive operation in ensuring international border controls and domestic quarantine are enforced.

Best Practices and Lessons Learned

Investment in the health system and UHC

Thailand has made significant investments in its healthcare infrastructure over the last 40 years—and most importantly by expanding rural health services across the country and broadening access to health centers at the community level. Throughout the pandemic, the Thai government has provided healthcare to all COVID-19 patients, and all patients have accessed treatment without any financial barriers through the three public insurance schemes, with almost 75% covered by the UHC. Building upon a relatively low cost but nationwide coverage of PHC has provided a solid foundation of and sustainability to the Thai UHC system, which helps buffer any adverse impacts of global health insecurity.

A strong public health system also allows for continuous risk assessment and active-case finding, even during the recovery period. After May 2020, Thailand actively conducted screening of at-risk populations including healthcare workers, public transportation workers, and migrants. Furthermore, VHVs have been identified as one of the critical components of the country's COVID-19 response.[39] Through door-to-door visits, healthcare education, and quarantine support, VHVs have helped minimize local transmission, raise awareness, and encourage compliance with disease control measures. The VHVs are also integral to the "Pattani New Normal Medical Services Model" in which patients are supported by remote consultation and medications for some conditions are refilled and home delivered by VHVs.[40]

Early response

Since the very first case of COVID-19 in January 2020, the Thai MOPH has shown strong leadership through coordinated efforts from various departments—including deploying existing field laboratories that have been crucial in making important, evidence-based decisions. As early as 4 January 2020, screening measures at points of entry were initiated by the Department of Disease Control, including preparing workforce and health facilities to respond to potential outbreaks. Early implementation of law enforcement through the Government Gazette

38   M. Bangprapa, and W. Nanuam. 2020. Every 'Phi Noi' from South Korea to Be Isolated. *Bangkok Post*. News release. 5 March.

39   WHO. 2020. Thailand's 1 million Village Health Volunteers - "Unsung Heroes" - are Helping Guard Communities Nationwide from COVID-19. News. 28 August. who.int/thailand/news/feature-stories/detail/thailands-1-million-village-health-volunteers-unsung-heroes-are-helping-guard-communities-nationwide-from-covid-19.

40   Thai Government Public Relations Department. 2020. *Successful Pattani Model on New Normal Medical Services to Be Expanded*. 25 June. https://thailand.prd.go.th/ewt_news.php?nid=9768&filename=index.

on 1 March 2020 as well as declaring COVID-19 as a dangerous communicable disease and an Emergency Decree on Public Administration was announced on 26 March. Partial lockdown measures were effective in disease control and dealing with cluster outbreaks and local transmissions (e.g., late night to early morning curfew, ban on international flights, 14-day mandatory quarantine for inbound passengers, and temporary closure of nonessential businesses).[41]

Holistic government approach and multisectoral collaboration

Under a state of emergency, establishment of the CCSA was also effective as the central response center for all public communications. Risk communication by the MOPH and daily press conferences by the CCSA's spokesperson provide essential up-to-date information to the public and advocate positive health behaviors, including early advice to encourage people to wear masks in public even before international health guidelines were announced.[42] The Thai government also leads a collaborative effort to crack down on dissemination of false information on COVID-19.[43]

Jointly developed with the Ministry of Digital Technology, the "Thai Chana" application platform helps to increase the capacity of contact tracing and case identification within the area. It works by requiring people to scan a QR code before entering and exiting premises (e.g., restaurants). For confirmed cases, investigation teams could then trace and follow-up contacts more easily. Another smartphone application, "DDC-Care," developed under Thailand's National Electronics and Computer Technology Center is designed to monitor symptoms of at-risk people using a 14-day self-screening online form (footnote 30). The MOPH continues to strengthen surveillance and laboratory capacity by providing trained epidemiologist teams, coordinating COVID-19

laboratory networks under its policy of "One Lab One Province, 24-hour Results," and facilitating private and public sector engagement (footnote 24).

Challenges and lessons learned

At the beginning of the outbreak, Thailand faced challenges with essential supply shortages. Several measures were implemented at the national level to address the problem. Following a Cabinet resolution on 4 February, the government designated four products—surgical facial masks, polypropylene, alcohol-based hand sanitizers, and toilet paper—as controlled goods, thereby making stockpiling and price gouging of these products illegal. The private sector and local manufacturers also applied technology to meet demand for PPE.

Due to limited health workforce capacity in rural areas, there were initial concerns around managing COVID-19 cases while still providing other essential healthcare services. However, the MOPH Department of Disease Control teams who were trained in field epidemiology and provincial public health offices have been able to provide essential support in case identification and contact tracing. Another vulnerable population subgroup during COVID-19 management relates to migrant workers. Over 10% of the total labor force is from neighboring countries—Cambodia, the Lao People's Democratic Republic (Lao PDR), Myanmar, and Viet Nam—accounting for an estimated 4 million documented and undocumented migrant workers.[44] Since early April, the Thai government has provided emergency support to migrant workers stranded in the country through UHC including those not covered under the Social Security System and the Migration Health Insurance Scheme.[45] The MOPH has implemented procedures for screening and surveillance of migrant workers

---

41   S. Dechsupa et al. Positive Impact of Lockdown on Covid-19 Outbreak in Thailand. *Travel Medicine and Infectious Disease.* 36. 101802.

42   J.N. Siewe Fodjo et al. 2020. Mass Masking as a Way to Contain Covid-19 and Exit Lockdown in Low- and Middle-Income Countries. *Journal of Infection.* 81 (3). pp. e1–e5.

43   C. Namwat et al. 2020. Thailand's Response against Coronavirus Disease 2019: Challenges and Lessons Learned. *Outbreak, Surveillance, Investigation & Response (OSIR) Journal* 13 (1). pp. 33–37.

44   UN Thematic Working Group on Migration in Thailand. 2019. *Thailand Migration Report 2019.* Bangkok: United Nations.

45   ILO. 2020. *Covid-19: Impact on Migrant Workers and Country Response in Thailand, July 2020.* ILO Country Office for Thailand, Cambodia, and the Lao PDR.

that will be traveling back to avoid potential spread of COVID-19.[46]

Discussion

COVID-19 has highlighted the importance of a responsive health system in mitigating the pandemic's impact. At the national level, the establishment of the CCSA has provided a focal point, as well as a **holistic government approach and coherent information to the public**. The MOPH has engaged in strong leadership through coordinated efforts from various departments including field laboratories that are crucial in making important, timely, and evidence-based decisions. **Health information and data management** between public and private sectors have contributed significantly to effective communication. Multisectoral collaboration and the development of innovative tools such as the "Thai Chana" and "DDC-Care" platforms help to increase the capacity of contact tracing and case identification for containing any outbreaks within different areas.

The Thai experience has benefited from **health security preparedness, a strong foundation of PHC, and investment in UHC**. Even before the implementation of UHC, Thailand had been investing in health infrastructure for decades, and the country's PHC facilities and hospitals were repurposed to accommodate COVID-19 patients, while maintaining other essential health services (footnotes 12 and 16). Existing health personnel and established networks in regional and local areas—notably, provincial health offices, PHC, and frontline VHVs—were able to support active-case finding, disease surveillance, and effectively reach out to people within the community with whom they had already formed a measure of trust.

One of the unique aspects of the Thai health system is the **health promotion initiative**. Initially proposed and coordinated between the MOPH and Ministry of Finance, the "sin tax" places a surcharge of 2% in excise taxes on tobacco and alcohol producers and importers.[47] ThaiHealth is an autonomous government agency established in 2001 and dedicated to promoting health literacy and health promotion activities. ThaiHealth has been a reliable source of COVID-19 information disseminated through traditional forms of media as well as social media.

The success of the Thai UHC is largely attributed to the health system reform, in which Prawase Wasi's "Triangle that Moves the Mountain"[48] conceptualized three components: (i) policy advocacy, (ii) social mobilization, and (iii) knowledge generation. In 1992, Thailand established two effective national research promotion and funding agencies: the Thailand Research Fund to support research capacity building and postgraduate training around health policy and systems; and the Health Systems Research Institute (HSRI), which provides evidence-based policies and was a main contributor to the development and success of the UHC. During the COVID-19 pandemic, the HSRI[49] has produced a range of technical reports with insights into innovations and household impacts.[50]

Furthermore, **public compliance** has been one of the most important elements of the fight against COVID-19. Strong public compliance with mandatory and voluntary preventative measures such as universal use of facial masks in public, social distancing precautions, remote working, and restricted nonessential venues have played an important role in stopping the widespread transmission of COVID-19.

---

[46] Department of Disease Control, Thai Ministry of Public Health. 2020. *Recommendations for Screening and Surveillance Procedures among Migrant Workers from Cambodia, Laos and Myanmar in Response to COVID-19.* 23 March. ddc.moph.go.th/viralpneumonia/eng/file/introduction/20Migrants.pdf.

[47] S. Pongutta et al. 2019. Lessons from the Thai Health Promotion Foundation. *Bulletin WHO.* 97 (3). pp. 213–220. https://doi.org/10.2471/BLT.18.220277.

[48] P. Wasi. 2000. "Triangle that Moves the Mountain" and Health Systems Reform Movement in Thailand. *Human Resources for Health Development Journal (HRDJ).* 4 (2). pp. 106–110.

[49] HSRI. 2020. *Health System Research Institute Forum: Stop Covid-19.* May. Nonthaburi.

[50] S. Pannarunothai. 2020. Surviving Covid-19 Pandemic with Knowledge and Action. *Journal of Health Systems Research.* 14. pp. 1–6.

Over the past 4 decades, Thailand has successfully implemented a number of public health campaigns including condom use for family planning and prevention of HIV/AIDs in the 1970s and 1980s.[51] Another major successful public health campaign aimed to combat NCDs through reducing health-risk behaviors (e.g., smoking, alcohol, and obesity) and promoting healthy behaviors (e.g., diet and physical activity). **The people's trust in the public health system, human resources for health, and financial protection through the UHC has provided confidence in accessing health services for testing and treatment for COVID-19.**

Conclusion

As of November 2020—and through the application of extensive measures, including early response and partial lockdown—Thailand has been able to contain the spread of COVID-19. The MOPH continues to strengthen surveillance and laboratory capacity, monitor data, share health information between government departments, and facilitate private and public sector engagement on vaccine research and distribution. The Thai people have adjusted well to a "new normal" lifestyle that includes social distancing, additional hygiene measures, mask wearing, and remote working for some businesses.

The impacts of COVID-19 are unprecedented not only on health systems but have also exposed vulnerabilities in the economy and society. Some international travel has resumed but the balance between boosting the economy and controlling the spread of the disease needs to be performed with caution.

The Ministry of Finance and Bank of Thailand have played crucial roles in mitigating the medium- and long-term economic impacts as well as implementing revival plans. Domestic travel subsidies for health workers and other Thais is an innovative way of boosting morale and stimulating the local economy. Amidst a slow global economy, a post COVID-19 recovery will require new holistic visions and strategies to aid employment, especially in tourism, the service sector, trade and agriculture sectors, as well as small and medium local businesses.

Until a vaccine is fully developed and distributed, Thailand will continue its strategy of interrupting transmission before major outbreaks occur. As the country continues, monitoring health impacts beyond physical health will be important, including mental health associated with stress and isolation and social impacts.

Overall, the Thai case study has highlighted and demonstrated the importance of health systems and the benefits gained from health security preparedness, a strong foundation and investment in PHC, and adoption of universal healthcare. Experience from previous decades in the development of the country's health systems and lessons learned from other countries in the Asia and Pacific region could contribute toward efforts in containing the current COVID-19 pandemic and other future emerging infectious diseases and mitigating any negative impacts.

---

[51] M. Viravaidya. 2007. From Family Planning to HIV/AIDS Prevention to Poverty Alleviation: A Conversation with Mechai Viravaidya. Interview by Glenn A. Melnick. *Health Affairs (Millwood)*. 26 (6). pp. w670–677.

3 Viet Nam

Executive Summary

Viet Nam has been held up by the global community as an exemplar of effective coronavirus disease (COVID-19) control despite having limited resources. As of 1 October 2020, there were 1,095 confirmed cases of COVID-19 and 35 deaths attributed to the disease in Viet Nam.[1] Viet Nam has invested heavily in its public health coverage system and health spending has outpaced the country's recent booming economic growth. As part of its commitment to achieving universal health coverage (UHC), Viet Nam has been moving toward building national emergency preparedness and response capacities to improve health security. This commitment, along with a system of stable financial resources for ongoing preventive activities, put the country in a strong position to deal with COVID-19.

Before a single case appeared in the country, the government issued guidance on the treatment of COVID-19, including instructing hospitals and clinics to prepare isolation and quarantine facilities in the event of an outbreak.[2] The government also acted decisively to issue a national response plan and set up response mechanisms, all while there were fewer than 10 cases reported nationally.[3] Additionally, measures such as closing schools, restricting large gatherings, and imposing mandatory quarantine among travelers returning from the People's Republic of China (PRC)

were also taken.[4] By 25 February 2020, there were 16 reported cases of COVID-19 in Viet Nam, most of whom had a travel history in the PRC. In March 2020, during the second phase of the outbreak, new cases initially rose due to importation from the Republic of Korea (ROK) and European countries, seeding clusters of local transmission. This prompted the government to impose its strictest set of countermeasures, which included suspending all international flights, mandating isolation for all international travelers, and closing nonessential services and businesses. The government also established a system of contact tracing linked to quarantine. By 22 April, the country had stabilized, with only 268 cases of COVID-19 reported. This marked the beginning of the third phase, during which Viet Nam experienced over 3 months with no local spread of disease.[5] In July, a resurgence of locally transmitted cases emerged in Da Nang and dramatically increased the number of cases during the first 2 weeks of August, with the total number of cases reaching 1,007 by 21 August 2020. By the end of August, however, the outbreak situation seemed to have been brought under control.

Viet Nam has avoided a major economic fallout due to the COVID-19 pandemic. As of the most recent economic projections, the country is one of the few economies in Asia and the Pacific not predicted to experience a contraction in 2020. A combination of existing financing mechanisms, individual economic

---

[1]   Center for Systems Science and Engineering (CSSE) at Johns Hopkins University. 2021. Coronavirus COVID-19 Dashboard. https://coronavirus.jhu.edu/map.html (accessed 1 October 2020).

[2]   Ministry of Health. 2020. *Decision No. 125/QĐ-BYT on Guideline for Diagnosis and Treatment for Novel Coronavirus Infection.* Viet Nam.

[3]   T. Phuong et al. 2020. Rapid Response to the COVID-19 Pandemic: Vietnam Government's Experience and Preliminary Success. *Journal of Global Health.* 10 (2). https://doi.org/10.7189/jogh.10.020502.

[4]   The Prime Minister. 2020. *The Official Dispatch No.156/CĐ-TTg on 2 February 2020 on Strengthening Prevention and Control of Acute Respiratory Infections Caused by New Stains of Corona Virus.* Viet Nam.

[5]   The Prime Minister. 2020. *Notice No. 158/TB-VPCP The Plan for Social Distancing from 16 April Across the Country.* Viet Nam.

support policies, and macroeconomic trends have so far allowed Viet Nam to achieve this success. In light of the country's efforts to minimize loss of human life and maintain economic productivity, a few strategies emerge that can help other countries emulate Viet Nam's experience:

- Aggressive preventive strategies employed quickly and decisively by the government kept widespread outbreaks from taking hold in the country.
- Rooted in its decentralized system, Viet Nam has been able to geographically wield nonpharmaceutical interventions, maximizing their impact while preserving economic activity as much as possible.
- Decisions to "protect health first" by, for example, restricting international tourism have prevented additional outbreaks and have actually translated into economic benefits as the country is projected to be the fifth-fastest growing economy in the world in 2020.[6]

Specific to COVID-19, Viet Nam provides concrete examples of effective strategies across all levels of pandemic response that can be replicated by other countries (e.g., testing, tracing, isolating, quarantining, nonpharmaceutical interventions, and providing nonhealth support). It is important to acknowledge that some measures taken by the country, such as government-mandated quarantine, may not work in other contexts. Still, the country's systemic response remains a model for other countries to learn from as they continue to refine responses to COVID-19 and preparations for future infectious disease outbreaks.

Introduction

Viet Nam was among the poorest countries in the world when it was unified in 1975. Today, the country is one of Southeast Asia's fastest growing economies and is a model for global development. Decades of economic reforms and a dedication to social welfare have left the country with a self-sufficient local economy, near universal literacy rates, and impressive

progress toward achieving UHC. These initiatives have put Viet Nam in a strong position to deal with external shocks, especially the COVID-19 pandemic. As the world struggles to contain COVID-19, countries across the globe are looking to Viet Nam to learn about the low-cost strategies that have been employed to keep loss of life and gross domestic product (GDP) at a minimum. An appreciation of the country's history and broader context helps to better understand how Viet Nam has leveraged its existing UHC infrastructure to combat COVID-19.

Background

Country context

With 96,462,110 inhabitants, Viet Nam—a Southeast Asian country—is ranked the 15th most populous country in the world.[7] The population is rapidly aging—in 2016, 11.9% of the population was over the age of 60 (compared with 7.1% in 1989).[8] It is expected that this number will increase 2.5 times by 2050, when almost one-in-five people will be elderly. About two-thirds of the country's population lives in rural areas, although this number is steadily decreasing (75% was rural in 2000). Viet Nam has 58 provinces and five municipalities under the central government. These five cities have populations of over 1 million, and the two largest cities, Ho Chi Minh City and Hanoi, have 8.5 and 7.5 million inhabitants, respectively. To the east, the country is bordered by the South China Sea, and to the north and west, Viet Nam shares 4,500 km of land borders with Cambodia, the Lao People's Democratic Republic, and the PRC. These extensive borders have tied Viet Nam's history and present fate to that of its neighboring countries.

Early economic and political reforms under "Doi Moi" focused on removing barriers to market liberalization and private sector development, ultimately allowing for private ownership of small enterprises and establishment of a national stock exchange. Equitable and widespread investment in education also helped sustain economic

---

[6]   World Bank Group. *Global Economic Prospects, June 2020*. http://hdl.handle.net/10986/33748.

[7]   World Bank. 2020. DataBank. https://databank.worldbank.org/home.aspx (accessed 5 September 2020).

[8]   Ministry of Health. 2017. *Joint Annual Health Review 2016: Towards Healthy Aging in Vietnam* (JAHR2016_Edraft).

progress and attract foreign investment.[9] These reforms have continued and, between 2002 and 2018, Viet Nam's GDP per capita increased by 2.7 times, lifting over 45 million people out of poverty, reducing poverty rates from over 70% to below 6% of the population.[10] In the midst of this period, Viet Nam progressed from one of the poorest countries in the world to middle-income status in 2010.[11] Today, the country is a single-party socialist republic which receives strong support from the population. Viet Nam is highly decentralized with a system of over 10,000 communes, each governed by an elected People's Council which is responsible for making socioeconomic development policies. These local structures are the backbone of Viet Nam's health system and have been crucial in delivering healthcare that meets local needs.

Health system

Over the past half-century, Viet Nam's life expectancy at birth has risen dramatically from 60 to 75 years. Improvements in maternal and child health have contributed to these advances. The country has already met and surpassed the Sustainable Development Goal (SDG) targets for maternal mortality ratio (SDG 3.1.1), proportion of births attended by skilled health personnel (SDG 3.1.2), under-5 mortality rate (SDG 3.2.1), and neonatal mortality rate (SDG 3.2.2) (footnote 7). Furthermore, the coverage of immunizations is generally high among the population, reflected by the fact that over 97% of children aged 12–23 months had been immunized for measles in 2018. The rising burden of noncommunicable diseases and rapid aging in the population pose challenges to the health system, which must adapt to meet the population's changing needs. Additionally, health outcomes are significantly worse than the national

average among disadvantaged groups, particularly among ethnic minorities and those living in the poorest or most remote provinces. While there is room for improvement, Viet Nam has made considerable progress in improving population health, which can be attributed to its commitment to public health systems.

Viet Nam has invested heavily in its public healthcare system, and health spending has outpaced the country's recent booming economic growth.[12] Since 2000, for every 1.0% increase in GDP per capita, public spending on health has increased by 1.7%.[13] This has translated into an almost three-fold increase of spending in constant US dollars, from $46.2 spent on health per capita in 2000 to $129.6 in 2017. During this time, the composition of health spending has not drastically changed. Out-of-pocket (OOP) expenditure and public health spending have both comprised about 40% of total health spending since 2000. Despite relatively large reliance on OOP spending, households are generally protected from catastrophic health expenditure, poverty related to OOP spending was low in 2017, at 1.3%.[14] Further, there is relative homogeny in health spending as a share of total household spending across income quintiles, indicating that OOP spending is not concentrated among the poor. Viet Nam's health investments have resulted in widespread coverage of the national social health insurance scheme.

A social health insurance scheme was introduced in Viet Nam in 1992; however, it did not cover much of the population until recently. Between 2000 and 2017, coverage in the scheme increased from 13% to 90% of Viet Nam's population.[15] Premium subsidies for poor and vulnerable households have contributed to increased coverage and healthcare utilization in

9   N.A. Nguyen and T. Nguyen. 2007. *Foreign Direct Investment in Vietnam: An Overview and Analysis of the Determinants of Spatial Distribution Across Provinces*. MPRA Paper 1921, University Library of Munich, Germany.

10 World Bank. 2020. Viet Nam Country Profile. https://www.worldbank.org/en/country/vietnam/overview (accessed 5 September 2020).

11 A. Baum. 2020. *Vietnam's Development Success Story and the Unfinished SDG Agenda. IMF Working Paper*. Working Paper No. 20/3. https://www.imf.org/en/Publications/WP/Issues/2020/02/14/Vietnam-s-Development-Success-Story-and-the-Unfinished-SDG-Agenda-48966.

12 WHO. 2020. *Global Health Expenditure Database*. https://apps.who.int/nha/database/country_profile/Index/en (accessed 5 September 2020).

13 H.S. Teo et al. 2019. *The Future of Health Financing in Vietnam: Ensuring Sufficiency, Efficiency, and Sustainability. World Bank Working Paper*. No. 139508. http://documents.worldbank.org/curated/en/222831563548465796/The-Future-of-Health-Financing-in-Vietnam-Ensuring-Sufficiency-Efficiency-and-Sustainability.

14 WHO. 2019. *Primary Health Care on the Road to Universal Health Coverage: 2019 Global Monitoring Report*. https://www.who.int/healthinfo/universal_health_coverage/report/uhc_report_2019.pdf.

15 Health Insurance Department. 2013. *Report on Results of Monitoring the Implementation of Health Insurance Policy and Law, Period of 2009–2012*. Hanoi: Vietnam Social Insurance; In Vietnamese.

Figure 3.1: Health System Organization in Viet Nam

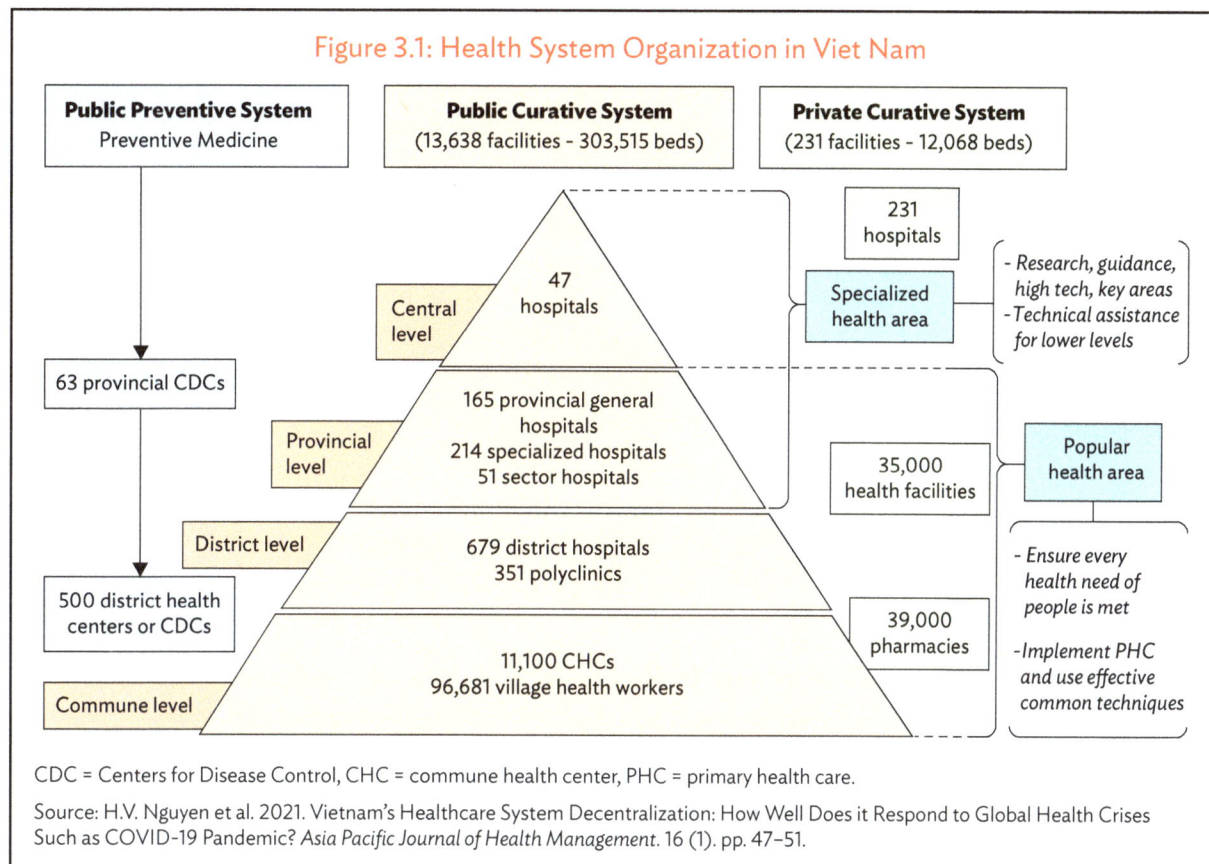

| **Public Preventive System** Preventive Medicine | **Public Curative System** (13,638 facilities - 303,515 beds) | **Private Curative System** (231 facilities - 12,068 beds) |

Central level — 47 hospitals

231 hospitals

Specialized health area
- Research, guidance, high tech, key areas
- Technical assistance for lower levels

63 provincial CDCs

Provincial level — 165 provincial general hospitals / 214 specialized hospitals / 51 sector hospitals

35,000 health facilities

Popular health area

District level — 679 district hospitals / 351 polyclinics

500 district health centers or CDCs

39,000 pharmacies
- Ensure every health need of people is met
- Implement PHC and use effective common techniques

Commune level — 11,100 CHCs / 96,681 village health workers

CDC = Centers for Disease Control, CHC = commune health center, PHC = primary health care.

Source: H.V. Nguyen et al. 2021. Vietnam's Healthcare System Decentralization: How Well Does it Respond to Global Health Crises Such as COVID-19 Pandemic? *Asia Pacific Journal of Health Management.* 16 (1). pp. 47–51.

poorer households.[16] Viet Nam's tiered health system infrastructure also helps to ensure that local needs are met. Healthcare facilities in the country are divided into four levels: central, provincial, district, and commune (Figure 3.1). Across these four levels, hospitals, health facilities, clinics, and community health workers are responsible for providing preventive and curative services for the population. Although higher-level hospitals have higher co-payments, local care options are often bypassed and overuse of hospital care is a significant challenge for the health system.[17] Another challenge is the fact that the health insurance scheme is operating at a deficit, and overspending may deplete the reserve fund as early as the end of 2020 (footnote 13). Still, the country has made great progress in ensuring financial protection through its social health insurance scheme which has contributed to substantial gains toward achieving UHC.

Relative to its level of income and its geographic neighbors, Viet Nam performs well in terms of progress toward UHC. The UHC service coverage index, developed by the World Health Organization (WHO) and World Bank to monitor progress toward coverage of health services, scores Viet Nam as 73 out of 100 (footnote 14). This score is higher than the average score both in its region (59 among Southeast Asian countries) and globally (64). As indicated previously, Viet Nam also performs well in terms of ensuring financial protection against high health spending. The incidence of catastrophic health expenditure has

[16]   T.V. Tien et al. 2011. A Health Financing Review of Viet Nam with a Focus on Social Health Insurance: Bottlenecks in Institutional Design and Organizational Practice of Health Financing and Options to Accelerate Progress Towards Universal Coverage. https://apps.who.int/iris/handle/10665/341160.

[17]   GSO (General Statistics Office) Vietnam. 2018. *Results of the Vietnam Household Living Standards Survey 2016.* Hanoi: Statistical Publishing House. https://www.gso.gov.vn/en/data-and-statistics/2019/03/result-of-the-vietnam-household-living-standards-survey-2016/.

reduced from 14.4% in 2006 to 9.4% in 2016 at the 10% threshold. Although efforts must still be made to improve health outcomes among the most vulnerable, improve efficiency of existing health spending, and address emerging health challenges, Viet Nam's health system has overall achieved impressive progress toward UHC at a low cost. As part of its commitment to achieving UHC, Viet Nam has been moving toward building national emergency preparedness and response capacities to improve health security.

Health security capabilities

A combination of factors makes Viet Nam susceptible to infectious disease outbreaks of human and zoonotic nature. The rapidly urbanizing population, high-risk livestock and wildlife farming practices, and extensive borders with active flows of trade, people, and goods have facilitated the emergence and spread of disease within the country. Since 2000, Viet Nam has suffered outbreaks of Severe Acute Respiratory Syndrome (SARS) in 2003, regular outbreaks of avian influenza (H5N1) during 2003–2012, and Zika virus in 2016.[18] This vast experience in handling outbreaks has helped the country strengthen its pandemic preparedness and response capacities.

Since 2005, Viet Nam has followed a national plan to implement the International Health Regulations (IHR 2005) under the guidelines of the Asia Pacific Strategy for Emerging Diseases. The country has since made steady progress in strengthening health security capacities as outlined under the IHR. In 2016, the country conducted a Joint External Evaluation (JEE) of these capacities and scored an average of 2.8 across all capacities—with 1 indicating no capacity and 5 indicating sustainable capacity. Almost all health security issues identified in the JEE technical areas are being addressed in Viet Nam. The Ministry of Health and the Ministry of Agriculture and Rural Development and their subordinate units are the main focal points for implementing health security activities at the central and provincial levels. Through their efforts, a total of $181 million was spent on health security activities across the 19 JEE technical areas in 2016.[19] The majority (73.8%) of this was spent at the provincial level, and spending varied widely between the 63 provinces, ranging from $280,000 in Bac Kan province to $12.9 million in Ho Chi Minh City. Despite differential levels of spending, financing for health security is secured, with several recurring budget and contingency mechanisms available in the country.

Health security, among other preventive measures, is prioritized in Viet Nam's budget allocation due to a party resolution that specifies that at least 30% of the total health budget must be allocated for preventive care.[20] The main source of funding for health security activities is the state budget, which includes recurrent budget line items, investment budgets (e.g., building laboratories and replenishing national reserves), budget allocated to national target programs, reserve budget funds (set at 2%–4% of the annual budget estimate) to be used in the case of emergency, along with other financial and national reserves. Importantly, Viet Nam has contingencies to ensure that reserve budgets are always allocated, available, and contain sufficient funding at district level, so that local officials have the flexibility and required resources necessary to mount a rapid response in the event of a public health emergency. This system of stable financial resources, for ongoing preventive activities, as approved and ensured by the Ministry of Finance, combined with additional reserve budgets for outbreaks proved to be useful in dealing with the 2003–2006 H5N1 outbreak.

In late 2003, H5N1 was first detected in poultry in Viet Nam and quickly spread to other poultry flocks and to humans. Between 2003 and 2006, there were three outbreaks of H5N1, resulting in the culling of 51 million poultry and economic losses of

---

[18]   WHO. 2020. *Disease Outbreak News: Viet Nam Country Profile.* https://www.who.int/emergencies/disease-outbreak-news (accessed 5 September 2020).

[19]   S. Osornprasop et al. 2019. *Health Security Financing Assessment for Viet Nam.* Vietnam Health Security Financing Assessment. World Bank.

[20]   National Assembly. 2017. *Resolution Of The Sixth Plenary Session The 12th Party Central Committee On The Protection, Care And Improvement Of People's Health In The New Situation.*

$176 million–$450 million.[21] To combat this outbreak, the government quickly formed a coordination framework, developed a national prevention plan and a national joint plan of action, and conducted coordinated simulation exercises to practice the implementation of these plans.[22]

Disease control measures included rapid identification followed by response to outbreaks, vaccination efforts in high-risk areas, and greater control and monitoring over poultry handling and transportation. Additional capacity building and awareness-raising activities were conducted to enhance government official and public knowledge on the disease. These activities were financed primarily by the contingency funds within the recurrent budget and supplementary budgets allocated for emergency response.

During the outbreak, provinces and municipalities were instructed by the Ministry of Finance to use local budgetary reserves and increase their budget revenues by aligning additional funds from the central budget to prevent and control the epidemic in their locality. Through these mechanisms, direct support was provided to households and firms as compensation for each lost bird and additional financial support was made available to prevent and respond to the disease at the local level (e.g., for improving infrastructure, procuring medical equipment and medicines, enhancing surveillance, conducting disease control measures, and implementing communications campaigns).

Major lessons learned from this outbreak include the following: (i) the importance of political commitment and leadership at all levels, (ii) ensuring stable and sustainable financial resources for ongoing activities works well to reduce the risk of outbreak and mobilize the entire system in the event of an emergency, (iii) pre-defined funds from contingency and reserve budgets enable financial preparedness for disease prevention and control, and (iv) timely and decisive actions are necessary and are enabled by mechanisms that ensure financial resources are available for rapid use.

Many of the lessons learned from combating the H5N1 outbreaks have been recognized and have translated to Viet Nam's successful measures to fight the COVID-19 pandemic.

COVID-19 in Viet Nam

Viet Nam has been held up by the global community as an exemplar of effective COVID-19 control with constrained resources. Although many researchers have described the lessons learned from Viet Nam's response to COVID-19, few have considered these within the broader context of the country's health and financing systems, particularly with regard to controlling disease outbreaks. This section describes the broad trends and key government actions during the various phases of the COVID-19 outbreak to date in Viet Nam, followed by a detailed analysis of various components of the response.

Overall transmission dynamics

As of 1 October 2020, there were 1,095 confirmed cases of COVID-19 and 35 deaths attributed to the disease in Viet Nam (also see footnote 1 on Chapter 1: Republic of Korea).

The transmission of COVID-19 in 2020 can be divided into five phases (Figure 2): Phase I (23 January–25 February) characterized by importation from other countries; Phase II (26 February–22 April) when new cases were a combination of importation and community infection; Phase III (23 April–24 July) during which the country experienced no local transmission and limited imported cases; Phase IV (25 July–4 September) when new community spread of disease occurred; and Phase V (4 September–1 October) when there has been no local transmission and limited imported cases.

When Chinese authorities first reported a case of COVID-19 to WHO on 31 December 2019, the Government of Viet Nam took note. Before a single case had appeared in the country, the Ministry of

---

[21] Ministry of Health, Ministry of Agriculture and Rural Development. 2011. The Viet Nam Integrated National Operational Program on Avian Influenza, Pandemic Preparedness and Emerging Infectious Diseases (AIPED) 2011–2015; A. McLeod et al. 2005. Economic and Social Impacts of Avian Influenza. Rome: FAO. http://www.fao.org/avianflu/conferences/rome_avian/documents/Economic-social-impact.pdf.

[22] World Bank. 2019. *Vietnam: A Case Study on Financing the Response to Avian Influenza H5N1 Outbreaks, 2003-06.*

Health had warned the public and government officials of an outbreak of unknown origin in the PRC and issued guidance on the treatment of COVID-19, including instructing hospitals and clinics to prepare isolation and quarantine facilities in the event of an outbreak in the country.[23] Viet Nam was among the first countries with a case of COVID-19, reporting its first imported cases of the disease on 23 January 2020.[24] By 1 February, travel to the PRC was drastically cut to limit importation because of COVID-19—all flights to and from the country were cancelled and the land border was also closed.[25]

The government also took decisive action to issue a national response plan, set up a Rapid Response Team and a National Steering Committee, and establish procedures for disease control, all while there were fewer than 10 cases reported nationally.[26] Additionally, strict measures were taken to reduce the spread of the disease including closing schools, restricting large gatherings, and imposing mandatory quarantines among travelers returning from the PRC.[27] The government also implemented the first targeted lockdown, closing the Son Loi Commune on 13 February (which had over one-third of all known cases in the country at the time). By 25 February, there were 16 reported cases of COVID-19 in Viet Nam, most of whom had a travel history in the PRC; however, effective quarantine and contact tracing measures prevented community transmission.

In the second phase of the outbreak, new cases initially rose due to importation from the ROK and European countries, which seeded clusters of local transmission. Cases steadily rose from 16 to 206 during March 2020. This prompted the government to impose its strictest set of countermeasures, which included suspending all international flights, mandating isolation for all international travelers, closing nonessential services and business, banning festivals and large gatherings, suspending the export of rice, and halting public transport in addition to targeted lockdowns in strategic areas.[28] A national epidemic was declared on 1 April. This flurry of government activity culminated in a directive that imposed a strict nationwide social distancing for 15 days which mandated self-isolation and only permitted leaving home for food and medicine.[29] These decisive actions had an immediate impact on reducing the local transmission of disease and, by 22 April, the country had stabilized at 268 cases (and 0 deaths) of COVID-19.

The government's decision to relax its social distancing campaign on 23 April ushered in the third phase, during which Viet Nam experienced over 3 months with no local spread of the disease.[30] The country retained strict quarantine-on-arrival measures for international travelers, yet this period was marked by a return to normal domestic activity. Schools were reopened, domestic flights were expanded, and the government promoted a campaign to encourage local tourism (footnote 28). This campaign, in combination with price cuts, led to a surge in domestic travel. Although 144 new cases were detected between 16 April and 24 July, these were all imported cases that

---

[23]   Ministry of Health. 2020. *Decision No. 125/QĐ-BYT on guideline for diagnosis and treatment for novel coronavirus infection.*

[24]   L.T. Phan et al. 2020. Importation and Human-to-Human Transmission of a Novel Coronavirus in Vietnam. *New England Journal of Medicine.* 382 (9). pp. 872–874. doi:10.1056/NEJMc2001272.

[25]   The Civil Aviation Authority of Vietnam. 2020. *Directive No. 362/CT-CHK - Prevention of Acute Respiratory Infections Caused by New Strains of Corona Virus to Aviation Activities in Vietnam.*

[26]   Ministry of Health. 2020. *Decision No. 1344/QĐ-BYT on Guideline for Diagnosis and Treatment for SARS-COV-2 (COVID-19);* The Prime Minister. 2020. *Directive No. 05/CT-TTg on Prevention and Control of Coronavirus Outbreak;* Ministry of Health. 2020. *Decision No. 255/QD-BYT on the Establishment of a Rapid Response Team to Control the Novel Coronavirus Disease (NCOV);* The Prime Minister. 2020. *Decision No. 170/QD-TTg on Establishment National Steering Committee for Control the Novel Coronavirus Disease.*

[27]   The Prime Minister. 2020. *The Official Dispatch No.156/CĐ-TTg on 2 February 2020 on Strengthening Prevention and Control of Acute Respiratory Infections Caused by New Strains of Corona Virus;* The Prime Minister. 2020. *Official Telegraph No.156/CĐ-TTg on Strengthening Prevention and Control of Acute Respiratory Infections Caused by New Strains of Corona Virus.*

[28]   T.P.T. Tran et al. 2020. Rapid Response to the COVID-19 Pandemic: Vietnam Government's Experience and Preliminary Success. *Journal of Global Health.* http://www.jogh.org/documents/issue202002/jogh-10-020502.htm.

[29]   The Prime Minister. 2020. Directive No. 16/CT-TTg—Implementation of social distancing nationwide; The Prime Minister. 2020. Directive No.15/CT-TTg on drastically implementing the peak phase of covid prevention.

[30]   The Prime Minister. 2020. Notice No. 158/TB-VPCP—The plan for social distancing from 16 April across the country.

tested positive when brought to quarantine facilities upon entering the country.[31] During this period, Viet Nam's strict quarantine procedures prevented community transmission of COVID-19 and enabled economic activity to resume. Further, the country remained vigilant with existing surveillance systems for influenza and respiratory infections and community and hospital event-based surveillance continuing to look for new cases. However, increased activity in the tourism-friendly city of Da Nang created a hotspot of transmission that challenged authorities.

On 25 July, a resurgence of locally transmitted cases emerged in Da Nang, first detected through the severe viral pneumonia surveillance platform, indicating the start of a new phase of outbreak. Within 3 days of this notification, nonpharmaceutical interventions were reimposed in selected provinces and districts, including bans on mass gatherings, school and work closures, stay-at-home orders, and restrictions on domestic travel. Surge capacity was built in Da Nang, the epicenter of the outbreak, through the deployment of a rapid response team and additional health workers, including establishment of a field hospital and an isolation facility, along with an expansion in testing capacity.[32]

The community outbreak affected 15 cities and/or provinces and dramatically increased infections during the first 3 weeks of August, with cases reaching 1,007 by 21 August. Unfortunately, during this phase, Viet Nam lost 32 lives to COVID-19. However, by the end of August, the outbreak situation seemed to be brought under control. Between 4 September and 1 October, there was no local transmission and limited imported cases. All signs indicate that Viet Nam has effectively combated another wave of infections, and is effectively detecting new cases at the border and preventing them from seeding new clusters of infection in the country. It is

therefore important to study the individual components of Viet Nam's pandemic preparedness and response system to understand the drivers of its success.

Detection

The entire Ministry of Health's approach to containing COVID-19 was centered on limiting active cases in the country to less than 1,000—the number of cases at which health facility capacity would begin to be overwhelmed. Since the beginning of the outbreak, Viet Nam has persistently applied measures to ensure early detection of disease, especially by endeavoring to test anyone in direct contact with infected individuals. Thanks to Viet Nam's extensive existing laboratory capacity, the country was able to isolate the virus that causes COVID-19, and culture it in a laboratory setting for research and manufacturing.[33] This facilitated the development of at least four locally validated and produced COVID-19 tests.[34] By June, there were at least 120 sites conducting community-based testing, and over 110 laboratories were able to analyze the results of any test, with a capacity of 27,000 samples per day.[35] The Ministry of Health also issued official guidelines on batch testing to increase capacity. In addition to rapidly ensuring testing capacity in the country, Viet Nam implemented various detection strategies in accordance with the epidemiologic situation at the time.

During the first two phases of disease transmission, when case numbers were relatively low, the country employed a strategy of testing all people arriving from abroad (once at the beginning and once at the end of quarantine) and testing cases and their immediate contacts to understand the extent of community spread. Through this strategy, as of 30 April, about 261,000 tests had been conducted, and Viet Nam had

31   WHO. 2020. *Viet Nam COVID-19 Situation Reports #1 and #2.* https://www.who.int/vietnam/emergencies/coronavirus-disease-(covid-19)-in-viet-nam/covid-19-situation-reports-in-viet-nam (accessed 1 October 2020).
32   K. Vu and P. Nguyen. 2020. Vietnam turns Danang Stadium into Field Hospital Amid Virus Outbreak. *Reuters.* https://www.reuters.com/article/us-health-coronavirus-vietnam-fieldhospi/vietnam-turns-danang-stadium-into-field-hospital-amid-virus-outbreak-idUSKCN2521B0 (accessed 1 October 2020).
33   L. Chau. 2020. *Vietnam Successfully Cultured and Isolated New Coronavirus Strain in Laboratory.* https://thanhnien.vn/thoi-su/viet-nam-phan-lap-duoc-virus-corona-gay-dich-viem-duong-ho-hap-cap-1179845.html (accessed 5 September 2020).
34   T. Pollack et al. 2020. Emerging COVID-19 Success Story: Vietnam's Commitment to Containment. *Our World in Data.* 30 June. https://ourworldindata.org/covid-exemplar-vietnam (accessed 5 September).
35   T.H.D. Nguyen. 2020. Lifting of Social Distancing Measures: Perspectives from Vietnam. *Disaster Medicine and Public Health Preparedness.* 15 (2). pp. E40–E42. doi:10.1017/dmp.2020.238.

the highest number of COVID-19 tests conducted per confirmed case in the world.[36] In the subsequent outbreak in Da Nang, testing was rapidly expanded, increasing by six-fold between the weeks of 19 July and 6 August.[37] The importance placed on testing during a community transmission scenario was highlighted when the government tested all 1.1 million inhabitants of Da Nang and all those who had returned from the city to other municipalities.[38] In addition to Viet Nam's COVID-19 testing strategy, existing infrastructure also played a major role in early detection, as the first cases of the Da Nang outbreak were identified through the country's severe viral pneumonia surveillance system. The coordination between detection systems and other processes helped to ensure that early detection resulted in containment measures that would stop the spread of disease.

Containment

Connected to its testing strategy, Viet Nam's containment measures are heavily reliant on contact tracing and have been extremely effective in preventing and mitigating community transmission of COVID-19. Once a case is confirmed, local public health officials work to identify and test any potential contacts that they could have infected in the past 14 days. If these contacts are positive, they are isolated at a hospital, and even if they test negative, they are quarantined at government-run quarantine centers (footnote 34). The government's decision to provide a daily allowance, in addition to other basic needs, was key to the success and adherence to quarantine procedures.[39] Contacts of the contacts of infected cases are placed in home-based isolation, and their contacts are also identified.

This system of tracing three degrees of contacts was facilitated by the launch of two government applications in particular: the GPS-based monitoring system in Hanoi (Hanoi Smart City) and the

"Bluezone" application, which helps users identify any close contact with a COVID-19 patient. Despite some concerns about privacy, these have been generally well received (over 25% of Viet Nam's 76 million smartphone users had downloaded the application as of 21 August 2020) and the overall rigorous strategy has helped to ensure that community spread is not occurring while maximizing limited testing resources.[40]

Quarantine plans developed at all levels during SARS and H5N1 influenza outbreaks were the foundation of Viet Nam's quarantine centers, and over 200,000 people were quarantined in government facilities between 23 January and 1 May (footnote 36). In addition to the official contact tracing strategy utilized by the Ministry of Health, other containment measures were effective in reducing the spread of disease.

Other notable containment strategies included the use of targeted lockdowns to keep as much of the economy functioning as possible. Between 13 February and 23 April, the country instituted at least eight localized lockdowns that included hospitals, individual streets, communes, and entire districts and affected anywhere between 150 and 10,000 people (footnote 34). During the second outbreak, only affected districts and provinces were subjected to nonpharmaceutical interventions. This ensured that containment measures were effectively targeted and always necessary.

Viet Nam's quarantine-on-arrival strategy ensured that visitors or returning citizens were isolated for 14 days upon entering the country. A government app, the "Vietnam Health Declaration," widely used to collect health information from both foreigners and Viet Nam nationals and determine their risk of exposure, facilitated quarantine and medical observation procedures. According to records from the Department of Preventive Medicine, all

---

36   T.Q. Pham et al. 2020. The First 100 Days of SARS-CoV-2 Control in Vietnam. *medRxiv* https://doi.org/10.1101/2020.05.12.20099242.

37   WHO. 2020. Viet Nam COVID-19 Situation Reports #1 and #3. https://www.who.int/vietnam/emergencies/coronavirus-disease-(covid-19)-in-viet-nam/covid-19-situation-reports-in-viet-nam (accessed 1 October 2020).

38   P. Nguyen and K. Vu. 2020. Vietnam's Danang to Test Entire Population as Outbreak Spreads Beyond City. *Reuters*. 1 August. https://www.reuters.com/article/us-health-coronavirus-vietnam-cases/vietnams-danang-to-test-entire-population-as-outbreak-spreads-beyond-city-idUSKCN24W39A.

39   Government of Vietnam. 2020. *Resolution No. 37/NQ-CP dated March 29, 2020 of the Government on Some Specific Regimes in Prevention and Control of the Covid-19 Pandemic.*

40   D. Nguyen. 2020. *Bluezone Covid-19 tracking app exceeded 20 million downloads. Vietnam Insider.* https://vietnaminsider.vn/bluezone-covid-19-tracking-app-exceeded-20-million-downloads/.

international and national border checkpoints had facilities and specialists available to conduct rapid patient diagnosis, quarantine, and treatment even before the COVID-19 outbreak (footnote 19). This existing infrastructure greatly facilitated the quarantine process and enabled the country to prevent hundreds of imported cases from seeding infections in the local community.

Treatment

Due in part to Viet Nam's strong UHC systems, COVID-19 patients are hospitalized free of charge, regardless of symptoms. Previous experience with the H5N1 outbreak prepared the country by conducting an inventory of the entire medical service system (e.g., total number of beds, capacity of emergency admissions, staff capacity, and equipment), enhancing the care services for influenza patients, upgrading health facilities and equipment (e.g., emergency rooms and ventilators), and conducting training for health workers (footnote 22).

In addition to these infrastructure investments, national guidelines for infection prevention and control were issued by the Ministry of Health on 19 February, which helped to prepare healthcare facilities to treat COVID-19 patients. A relatively small number of cases were reported among health workers: four cases from 23 January to 30 April, and 34 cases between 23 July and 27 August. Still, the high number of health worker infections (4% of all infections as of 31 August) is relatively high.

A February study on healthcare worker attitude toward COVID-19 in a Ho Chi Minh City hospital found that about one-third of workers did not know the mode of transmission, recommended isolation period, or best practice treatments.[41] Follow-up studies are needed to determine if this changed over time, but additional guidance could be necessary to protect this high-risk population from infection.

The government has done well to identify and protect certain high-risk groups. Viet Nam is a rapidly aging country and, given that COVID-19 is more severe in elderly populations, special measures must be taken to prevent them from suffering disproportionally. In addition to issuing guides to managing the health of the elderly and those with chronic diseases, youth organizations worked to provide social support and free food to elderly individuals in certain provinces.[42] This example of social solidarity points to the larger cohesion that enhanced disease control measures in the country.

Risk communication and community engagement

Absolutely essential to Viet Nam's successful COVID-19 response are the combination of clear, transparent messaging along with the population's high level of engagement and buy-in.

As early as 30 January, the government directed the Department of Health to coordinate with communications stakeholders to launch communications campaigns at the province, district, and commune levels to proactively prevent and combat new infections.[43] This was implemented by the Ministry of Information and Communications through text messages for mobile subscribers; enhancing communication and collaboration between hospitals and health facilities; newspaper, radio, and television campaigns; social media awareness-raising (including promptly identifying and correcting "fake" news); and producing videos and films to circulate anti-COVID-19 information, especially on social media.[44] One of these short videos, produced in collaboration between the Ministry of Health and a local artist, went viral globally and became a popular rallying point for engaging young people in COVID-19 prevention.[45]

---

[41] G. Huynh et al. 2020. Knowledge, Attitude, and Practices Regarding Covid-19 among Chronic Illness Patients at Outpatient Departments in Ho Chi Minh City, Vietnam. *Risk Management and Healthcare Policy* 3. pp. 1571–1578. doi: 10.2147/RMHP.S268876.

[42] L.T. Tung. 2020. Social Responses for Older People in COVID-19 Pandemic: Experience from Vietnam. *Journal of Gerontological Social Work.* 63 (6–7). pp. 682–687. doi: 10.1080/01634372.2020.1773596.

[43] Ministry of Health. 2020. *Official Dispatch No. 369/BYT-TT-KT on Strengthening Propaganda, Advocacy of Prevention and Control of nCoV.*

[44] Ministry of Information and Communications. 2020. *Directive No. 5/CT-BTTTT on Prevention and control of COVID-19.*

[45] *British Broadcasting Corporation.* Coronavirus: Vietnam's Handwashing Song Goes Global. https://www.bbc.com/news/av/world-asia-51764846.

The Ministry of Health also launched a COVID-19-specific website and assisted in the development of several applications, all of which serve as platforms to directly communicate information with the public. In some communes, loudspeakers, originally placed to warn communities about enemy operations and potential bomb drops during wartime, have been used to broadcast messages on COVID-19 prevention twice daily.[46] This innovative and low-cost information sharing system has allowed for timely dissemination of messages at a local level, even among those who may not have access to smartphones and other technology.

In addition to these platforms, Viet Nam's political and social leaders have been consistent and coordinated in presenting the gravity of the COVID-19 situation and the need to observe and obey official guidance as a matter of national pride.[47] In return, public support for the government and adherence to these measures has been among the best in the world.

Multiple surveys have found that Vietnamese have great confidence in the government response to COVID-19. A survey in early April found that 97.1% of Vietnamese respondents perceived the government to be truthful in messaging, and 95% believed that the government response was sufficient to end the spread of disease.[48] These equated to the second highest belief in government messaging and the third highest belief that government response was sufficient across the 58 countries surveyed. Further, the same survey indicated that Vietnamese respondents had the highest belief in the effectiveness of social distancing measures to slow the spread of COVID-19.

These findings were corroborated by a second study conducted in May, which found that 89% of Vietnamese respondents "completely" or "somewhat" trusted the media, and 97% trusted the government's handling of the epidemic.[49] This high level of confidence in the truthfulness of messaging and the competency of government has translated to high overall levels of compliance with and adherence to COVID-19 preventive measures among the Vietnamese population, including almost universal (99.5%) adherence to face mask use when outdoors.[50]

Although some aspects of government measures may infringe upon individual liberties (e.g., tracking GPS location of confirmed cases and mandatory quarantines for contacts), the Vietnamese people have largely approved of government response to COVID-19 and are adhering to official guidance on infection prevention. The combination of strong, consistent messaging combined with unrelenting public support has made Viet Nam's risk communication and community engagement a true model of success.

Financing

Viet Nam has avoided major economic losses due to the COVID-19 pandemic. As of June, Viet Nam is one of the few economies in Asia and the Pacific not predicted to experience a contraction in 2020. The country's forecast GDP growth of 1.8% for 2020 and 6.3% for 2021 show promising signs for the country's economy.[51] A combination of existing financing mechanisms, individual economic support policies, and macroeconomic trends have so far allowed Viet Nam to achieve this success.

The country accessed its contingency fund (5% of funds from the 2020 budget) set aside for use in emergency, allowing for immediate response at central and local levels without any borrowing. Additionally, the country was able to absorb some of the shock due to lower revenue because of its accumulation of reserves. This prudent fiscal management, before the pandemic even started, gave Viet Nam a head start

[46]   P. Dung and H. Nguyen. 2020. Participating in Prevention of Epidemic COVID-19: The Ward Speaker Spoke Again. *Lao Dong*.

[47]   M. Trevisan, L.C. Le, and A.V. Le. 2020. The COVID-19 pandemic: a view from Vietnam. *American Journal of Public Health* 110. pp. 1152–1153. https://ajph.aphapublications.org/doi/full/10.2105/AJPH.2020.305751.

[48]   T. Fetzer et al. 2020. Global behaviors and perceptions in the COVID-19 pandemic. *PsyArXiv*. https://doi.org/10.31234/osf.io/3kfmh.

[49]   YouGov. 2020. International COVID-19 tracker. https://today.yougov.com/covid-19 (accessed 1 October 2020).

[50]   N.P.T. Nguyen et al. 2020. Preventive behavior of Vietnamese people in response to the COVID-19 pandemic. *PLoS ONE* 15 (9). e0238830. https://doi.org/10.1371/journal.pone.0238830.

[51]   ADB. 2020. *Asian Development Outlook 2020 Update: Wellness in Worrying Times*. https://www.adb.org/publications/asian-development-outlook-2020-update.

in financing response operations and gave local and central authorities much-needed flexibility during the crucial early days of the outbreak.

Still, the economic impacts were severe, as over 30 million Vietnamese workers, totaling half of the country's workforce, were affected during the height of the lockdown in April.[52] In response, the country cut taxes on essential goods (e.g., medical supplies) and electricity, gave extensions on tax and rent payments, restructured loans to provide support to individuals affected by COVID-19 ($2.6 billion through Resolution No. 42/ND-CP), and supported businesses in recovery ($10.7 million through Resolution No. 42/ND-CP) (footnote 3). Despite these positive actions, Viet Nam's GDP growth for 2020 is down by over 5% compared to 2019 and 2018, suggesting that the government could have introduced additional fiscal stimulus to combat the massive impact on individuals and micro-, small-, and medium-size enterprises.

The pandemic has been especially harmful to the services industry, which has been heavily impacted by the lack of international tourism. Viet Nam's diverse domestic economic activity, especially in agroforestry and fisheries, has ensured that economic growth will persist, albeit at a much lower rate, through this crisis. Although Viet Nam's health-related successes in COVID-19 response have garnered international acclaim, its economic achievements are arguably as impressive and deserve more attention.

Leadership

One of the key factors driving Viet Nam's overall success is the early and persistent commitment of high-level leaders to combat COVID-19. As early as 27 January, Viet Nam's Prime Minister Nguyen Xuan Phuc made an address about COVID-19, making the decision to prioritize health and saving lives over the economy and calling for the nation to "fight the epidemic as an enemy." He also called for the establishment of the National Steering Committee to coordinate the country's response, chaired by Deputy

Prime Minister Vu Duc Dam. Importantly, this steering committee involved high-level members from a wide range of stakeholders, whose roles and responsibilities were largely delineated and understood before the pandemic started.

Viet Nam's existing pandemic preparedness plans have accompanying operational plans that denote which ministries are responsible for which actions in the event of a disease outbreak (footnote 21). Credit must be given to the national leadership and the Ministry of Health for their wide range of prompt, proactive, and decisive responses to mobilize and improve healthcare systems, protect the country from imported disease, implement evidence-based nonpharmaceutical interventions, develop a creative communications campaign to engage public support, and provide economic relief (footnote 3).

These centrally coordinated responses were also successfully implemented at local levels thanks to Viet Nam's strong decentralized health system structure. Of note, local implementation of targeted lockdowns and business closures has meant that the country has been able to minimize interruptions to economic activity in unaffected areas, a major factor in mitigating economic losses due to the pandemic. The country gives an example for how strong central leadership and precise interventions supported by local implementers can mitigate the impact of COVID-19.

Cross-sector Cooperation

Pandemic preparedness and response requires a multisectoral approach and Viet Nam has taken strong steps to mitigate disruptions across society. One example is seen in the government's assurance of food security, which has previously been an issue in the country. In March, Viet Nam stopped exporting rice to ensure sufficient domestic supply. By the time exports were resumed in May, global rice prices were 40% above their year-earlier levels, which came with great benefits to farmers and the overall economy.[53]

---

52   World Bank. 2020. What will be the New Normal for Vietnam? The Economic Impact of COVID-19.
53   Food and Agriculture Organization of the United Nations. 2020. *Global Information and early Warning System on Food and Agriculture— Viet Nam Country Brief*. 21 August.

Also important to Viet Nam's pandemic preparedness and response systems is the incorporation of a "One Health" approach, which recognizes that the health of humans, animals, and the environment are deeply interconnected (footnotes 21 and 53). Incorporating animal health authorities, and giving the Ministry of Agriculture and Rural Development a leading role in pandemic preparedness and response enables a comprehensive approach to dealing with zoonotic diseases, and certainly facilitated the study and prevention of cross-over events when the disease's transmission routes were unknown.[54] Having stakeholders from other sectors involved in response also helps mitigate the economic and societal impact of the pandemic.

The tourism sector, which comprises almost 10% of GDP, is losing an estimated $1 billion each month (footnote 52). Involving officials from the Viet Nam Ministry of Culture, Sports, and Tourism in pandemic response ensures that steps are taken to recover the important sector, while not sacrificing health gains. Other gains made to accrue human capital must also not be lost due to COVID-19 prevention measures. Researchers are studying the impact of school closures on student learning and the education system, which have largely transitioned to online platforms.[55] More data and experiences will emerge over time on the impacts of COVID-19 and mitigation strategies utilized across various sectors; however, it is encouraging that the government is coming from a whole-of-society approach to pandemic preparedness and response.

Best Practices and Lessons Learned

Viet Nam's successes in COVID-19 response are far-reaching. Others have already pointed to the country's strong government leadership, comprehensive preparation, effective multisectoral collaboration and coordination, and effective risk communications and community engagement campaigns.[56] These are certainly to be commended. In light of the country's ability to minimize loss of human life, and maintain economic productivity, a few principles and strategies emerge that can help other countries mirror Viet Nam's success.

Prevention is better than cure

This motto is ubiquitous in Viet Nam's society, and it has been formalized and adopted both into the organization of its health system and its approach to pandemic response. Mandated by law, 30% of health spending must be toward preventive measures, and the public preventive system is an explicitly defined and operational part of the health system. The country's investment in and commitment to preparation for disease outbreaks (e.g., developing operational plans for response, performing simulation exercises to test plans, financing pandemic preparedness capacities, and ensuring contingency budgets for emergency) ensured that national and local responses were organized, coordinated, and premeditated. A 2016 analysis showed that over half of all government financing for health security was allocated to prevention measures, with far less allocated to building detection and response (footnote 19). Aggressive preventive strategies employed quickly and decisively by the government (e.g., three degrees of contract tracing with appropriate quarantine and isolation, quarantining visitors on arrival, and maintaining vigilant surveillance) have enabled widespread outbreaks from ever taking hold in the country. In fact, as of 27 August, over one-third of provinces had not yet reported a single case of COVID-19. This has enabled the government to target resources to key areas, avoid crippling

---

[54] United States Agency for International Development (USAID). 2020. *USAID Helps Vietnam Improve its COVID-19 Laboratory Testing Capacity.* https://www.usaid.gov/vietnam/program-updates/mar-12-2020-usaid-helps-vietnam-improve-its-covid-19-laboratory-testing-capacity.

[55] T. Trung et al. 2020. Dataset of Vietnamese student's learning habits during COVID-19. *Data in Brief.* 30. 105682.

[56] B.T.T. Ha et al. 2020. Combating the COVID-19 Epidemic: Experiences from Vietnam. *International Journal of Environmental Research and Public Health* 17 (9). 3125; H. Quach, and N. Hoang. 2020. COVID-19 in Vietnam: A Lesson of Pre-Preparation. *Journal of Clinical Virology* 127. 104379; S.M. Le. 2020. Containing the Coronavirus (COVID-19): Lessons from Vietnam. https://blogs.worldbank.org/health/containing-coronavirus-covid-19-lessons-vietnam.

nationwide lockdowns, and ensure that health systems are not overwhelmed by an influx of cases.

Using a scalpel instead of a sledgehammer

Rooted in its decentralized system of governance, Viet Nam has been able to geographically target nonpharmaceutical interventions to maximize the impact of interventions while preserving economic activity as much as possible. Since the beginning of the outbreak, the country has not hesitated to put specific buildings, streets, or communes under lockdown to prevent further disease transmission. Similarly, placing close contacts under government quarantine has been an effective way to prevent asymptomatic spread of the disease. These targeted measures may help maintain public trust in the government's response and in the efficacy of nonpharmaceutical interventions, which will be important in a protracted pandemic scenario. Additionally, focusing testing efforts on populations with community transmission (e.g., the city of Da Nang), and any close contacts of those who test positive, helps epidemiologists to understand the scope of outbreaks and increases the efficiency of resources compared to widespread testing without a strategy. In the likely situation that the pandemic continues in subsequent waves of infection, continuing this targeted approach will be important to minimize disruptions to society while maximizing the impact of interventions.

Putting people's health first

Early in the outbreak, Prime Minister Nguyen Xuan Phuc made the bold decision to unequivocally prioritize the health of his people, saying he was "willing to sacrifice some economic benefits to protect people's lives."[57] Decisions to restrict international tourism, while harmful for the economy, have avoided additional outbreaks from being seeded. While the government has certainly taken measures to mitigate economic impacts, the effects of protecting health first have actually translated into economic benefits. First, Viet Nam's external sector is thriving, as exports were up by 5% and over $12 billion of foreign direct investment was registered during the first quarter of 2020.[58] Due to low infection rates and the lack of nationwide lockdowns, Viet Nam was still able to produce exports and maintain confidence to invest in the country. Second, using the statistical value of life, the dollar value of lives saved can be estimated at around $15 billion, far higher than the forecast total loss of GDP in 2020 (footnote 52). By committing to saving lives first, Viet Nam has actually reinforced its economic position, and the country is projected to be the fifth fastest-growing economy in the world in 2020.[59]

Discussion

Specific to COVID-19, Viet Nam provides concrete examples of effective strategies across all levels of pandemic response that can be replicated by other countries (e.g., testing, tracing, isolating, quarantining, nonpharmaceutical interventions, and providing nonhealth support). It is important to acknowledge that some measures taken by the country, especially government-mandated quarantine and location-tracking apps, may not work in other contexts that place a premium on personal liberties. However, the fact that Viet Nam's population remains so supportive of its government and the response indicates that these sacrifices are deemed appropriate. Further, Viet Nam's response has been so successful because interventions have been coordinated and adapted to meet the epidemiological situation of the country. For example, the country's targeted lockdowns and outbreak investigation measures would not work in a context where there was nationwide community transmission that overwhelmed contact tracing infrastructure. The intensive three-degree contact tracing system might not have been as effective in preventing asymptomatic spread if it was not linked

57   How Vietnam Sacrifices Economy to Protect Its People? *Hanoi Times.* 2020. http://hanoitimes.vn/how-vietnam-sacrifices-economy-to-protect-its-people-311354.html (accessed 8 September 2020).

58   J. Morisset. 2020. Vietnam: A Bright Star in the COVID-19 Dark Sky. *World Bank Blogs.* 28 May. https://blogs.worldbank.org/eastasiapacific/vietnam-bright-star-covid-19-dark-sky.

59   World Bank Group. 2020. *Global Economic Prospects, June 2020.* https://www.bancomundial.org/es/news/press-release/2020/06/08/covid-19-to-plunge-global-economy-into-worst-recession-since-world-war-ii.

to a mandatory quarantine, likewise the government-mandated quarantine may not have been as well received had there not also been provisions for daily stipends. However, the country's systemic response remains a model for other countries to learn from as they continue to refine responses to COVID-19 and preparations for future infectious disease outbreaks.

The world is currently solidly in the "panic" phase in the cycle of panic and neglect related to interest in pandemics and pandemic response. Although calls to break this cycle have largely fallen on deaf ears, Viet Nam's COVID-19 experience is perhaps the most concrete evidence in favor of the benefits of investing in pandemic preparedness and overall preventive capacities in health systems during times of peace. Annual spending of less than $2.00 per capita on health security capacities has been enough to adequately prepare the country to mount one of the best responses to COVID-19 in the world (footnote 19). Given that the COVID-19 pandemic is estimated to cost the global economy between $5.8 trillion and $8.1 trillion, it would take over 1,000 years of global health security investment at this level before preventive spending outweighed the losses from COVID-19.[60] Countries must follow Viet Nam's lead and scale up and maintain investments in health security capacities, especially during the periods when they are not fighting disease outbreaks.

In addition to health security, Viet Nam's experience demonstrates the need for a paradigm shift in overall health systems from curative to preventive services. Viet Nam's emphasis on preventive care as a distinct component of its larger health system provides a solid platform for pandemic response to build on. However, investments in preventive care can also yield returns during inter-pandemic periods. As noncommunicable diseases comprise a larger percent of the global burden of disease, comprehensive primary care systems that are skilled in preventive medicine will increasingly become cost-effective methods of delivering population health. Strategies to sustainably finance and incentivize these shifts must also be adopted. Viet Nam's mandated 30% of budget spent on preventive healthcare is an excellent start toward a preventive health system. These preventive services should be covered within the essential package of services under UHC strategies. Adopting metrics to evaluate health systems in terms of their ability to provide preventive services can further help incentivize countries to prepare for emerging health systems challenges. As demonstrated by Viet Nam, prevention is truly better than cure.

Conclusion

In the first week of October, Viet Nam reported fewer than five new cases per day, all of which were imported. It looks as though the Da Nang outbreak has been fully brought to heel by the country's rapid and decisive containment measures. Time will tell whether the country will return to the lack of community transmission experienced from late April to July, or whether calls to reopen the country to international tourists will result in new infections and outbreaks. Looming factors, like the introduction of a vaccine, will further complicate the global COVID-19 situation. Viet Nam is included in the COVID-19 Vaccines Global Access Advance Market Commitment, but hard decisions about allocation, delivery, and securing additional vaccines lie ahead. By staying committed to the principles of prevention over cure, implementing targeted control measures where necessary, and valuing human life, Viet Nam can maintain high levels of public trust while meeting these new challenges and continue to keep COVID-19 at bay.

[60]   ADB. 2020. *An Updated Assessment of the Economic Impact of COVID-19.* http://dx.doi.org/10.22617/BRF200144-2.

What Have We Learned from These Countries?

Despite different demographics, fiscal space, health systems, and governance structures, each of the three countries studied demonstrated success in responding effectively to COVID-19 in one area or another—with valuable examples of key actors working together for a common goal. In all three, nationwide efforts to curb transmission of the virus have been widely considered successful thus far—with country caseloads and total deaths remaining remarkably low nearly 1 year after the pandemic began. These achievements cannot be overstated in light of the global reality, where many countries with the same, or more, resources have struggled to contain spread of the virus.

Considering that every country in the world has been affected by the pandemic, these case studies reflect a number of rich insights and good practices that apply beyond their specific contexts and even beyond the current pandemic. Thus, they may prove valuable to other countries as they move through different phases of their pandemic response.

Taken as a whole, the three case studies offer the following lessons learned and good practices.

Investing in preventative and public health protects populations and economies

Evidence from across the world has demonstrated that investments in public health systems have been critical in responding effectively to COVID-19 and mitigating economic shocks. These cases are no exception. All three countries—the ROK, Thailand, and Viet Nam— have adopted UHC and invested heavily in primary and preventive health infrastructure, including health worker capacity, and pandemic preparedness.

These investments, largely made over decades, have undoubtedly contributed to their low total number of cases and deaths. Although few countries have escaped recession, economies across the world are poised to recover, while the loss of life cannot be undone.

Adopting a flexible emergency response framework enables countries to adapt to rapidly changing conditions

All three countries executed flexible, adaptive, and timely responses to unique or shifting circumstances. For example, after experiencing a surge in cases in Daegu that threatened to overwhelm health systems, the ROK quickly reorganized its patient classification system to more efficiently allocate resources to patient care. Viet Nam, too, quickly tailored their detection strategies in accordance with a shifting epidemiologic situation. When caught off-guard by a fresh outbreak of the virus in the tourist area of Da Nang, after nearly 100 days without a single confirmed case of local transmission, the government quickly set out to test all 1.1 million of the city's inhabitants. These targeted measures were supported by strong pandemic preparedness frameworks and resulted in effective responses that stemmed outbreaks before large-scale lockdowns were required.

Using real-time, rigorous data is critical for the roll-out of targeted, context-specific models

The use of data to provide real-time visibility of outbreaks at the community level was instrumental to the success in all three contexts. From the ROK's aggressive use of digital health data and data analytics, Viet Nam's third-degree contact tracing system, and Thailand's deployment of existing field laboratories, all three countries exercised the use of data as a primary tool to understand how the virus was spreading and where hotspots would emerge. Furthermore, all of the countries employed the use of various data tracking systems (e.g., dashboards, data maps, and alerting systems) to create an actionable picture of virus activities. These data-driven efforts proved crucial for monitoring and managing various outbreaks in certain outbreak settings.

Incorporating communities in design and implementation contributes significantly to overall response efforts

Through a number of strategic efforts, community action strengthened coronavirus response across all three contexts. In many cases, community actors served as catalysts for the design and implementation of effective measures to stem the virus. For example, in Thailand, massive cadres of community health workers and volunteers were deployed to support specific elements of the response. This included supporting prevention efforts through its network of more than a million village health volunteers. In the ROK, civil society and community groups identified gaps in care, monitored vulnerable populations, and provided additional disaster relief support.

In Viet Nam, during targeted lockdowns, volunteers provided meals and other essentials to vulnerable populations. But perhaps the Vietnamese population's almost universal (99.5%) adherence to face mask use when outdoors is the most vivid example of the effectiveness of community action in preventing the spread of the virus. Building on lessons learned from previous disease outbreaks, such as Ebola, the importance of engaging communities and developing culturally-sensitive response measures has again proven to be a key facilitator in the successful management of a public health crisis.

The Way Forward

We are still in the midst of a pandemic. Although there is much more work to be done by countries around the world to strengthen and reinforce the foundations of pandemic preparedness and response, these three case studies illuminate some of what has worked thus far. One element that emerges across these cases and the others highlighted in this document is the importance of a whole-of-government and whole-of-society approach to pandemic response.

The success of the majority of the good practices identified here hinges on cooperation and collaboration of multiple stakeholders, both public and private, at national and local levels. Pandemic preparedness and response cannot be managed by public health officials alone.

Coordinated response across and within key sectors including finance, transportation, communication, and health ministries is needed in addition to support from the highest level of government and private sector entities. This coordination is particularly important as countries continue to recover from the far-reaching impacts of the pandemic and certainly as national-level planning shifts to vaccine delivery.

These case studies clearly demonstrate that prevention through deliberate actions to strengthen primary healthcare systems, including progress toward UHC, is a worthwhile investment. These investments, if made continuously over time, result in improved responses during health emergencies.

Countries emerging from the COVID-19 pandemic must commit to the principle that preparedness and prevention are far better, and far less costly, than response. ADB remains committed to supporting developing member countries in applying these and other lessons moving forward so that they can contribute to a more resilient Asia and the Pacific.

www.ingramcontent.com/pod-product-compliance
Lightning Source LLC
Chambersburg PA
CBHW050054220326
41599CB00045B/7409